Becoming Family

Becoming Family

by

Jeanette Benson
and Jack L. Hilyard

Saint Mary's Press
Christian Brothers Publications • Winona, Minnesota

to those who continually define family
for us:

our parents and families
and
our communities

ACKNOWLEDGMENTS

Selections from *Peoplemaking* by Virginia Satir. Copyright © 1972 by Science and Behavior Books, 1972. Used by permission of Science and Behavior Books, Inc.

Selections from *Making Contact* by Virginia Satir. Copyright © 1976 by Virginia Satir. Reprinted with permission of the publisher, Celestial Arts, 231 Adrian Road, Millbrae, CA 94030.

Reference to *Pezzettino* by Leo Lionni. Used with permission of Pantheon Books, A Division of Random House, Inc.

Selections from "The Johari Window" by Joseph Luft. Published in *Human Relations Training News*, Volume 5, Number 1, 1961. Copyright © 1961 by NTL Institute. Reproduced by special permission of NTL Institute.

Cover illustrator: Elizabeth M. Nelson

Contents

IV. Appendices

Foreword

This is a very serious book about improving and illuminating family relationships. It amply demonstrates that learning new approaches toward very serious subjects can be fun.

The content of the book speaks to our mind, heart, feelings, senses, body, soul, and interrelationships to others.

A central portion of the book presents a well-rounded and comprehensive series of exciting, colorful, and non-threatening games and exercises, each of which has a profound point as its aim.

The authors establish a context in which people can enter into potentially threatening areas of family life with a spirit of enthusiasm and experimentation.

The message throughout the book is: try out these fascinating, appealing games and exercises and see what can be learned from them.

The directions for the exercises are clearly spelled out and presented in such a creative way that one can literally and figuratively understand the aim.

I heartily recommend this book.

Virginia Satir, D.S.S.

Acknowledgments

We offer special thanks to:

those persons who have worked with us and who have helped to shape our lives and

those persons who have shared their vision of education through and with multi-family groups.

In particular we are grateful to:

our families and communities, who have given us love;

Margaret Sawin, who shared a vision of a pathway toward the concept of family cluster;

Virginia Satir, who continually clarifies the vision through her life and message;

Joe Beno and the parish of Sacred Heart in Medford, Oregon, who risked for the vision;

Lynn Young and the training community in the Episcopal Diocese of Olympia, who shared training skills.

And special thanks to those who helped in the preparation of this manuscript:

the many families who have shared their experience in the shaping of the exercises;

Jane Lord and Jane Hilyard, for the design of the family figures that have become a symbol of our work;

Mary Gleason, for the personal and professional care she offered us and this manuscript;

Brother Alphonsus Pluth, for his encouragement, patience, and editorial critique.

I Beginning

CHAPTER 1

Stems

Are You Looking For . . .

a <u>spark</u> to help you design for your needs, your families, your situation?

help in working with a TEAM?

HELP in working with families?

|||// IDEAS to work from?

a book on **FAMILY** education?

a book you can use <u>with</u> your family?

HELP FOR SINGLE PARENT FAMILIES?

a way to SHARE values with families?

a new experience?

This Book Is About . . .

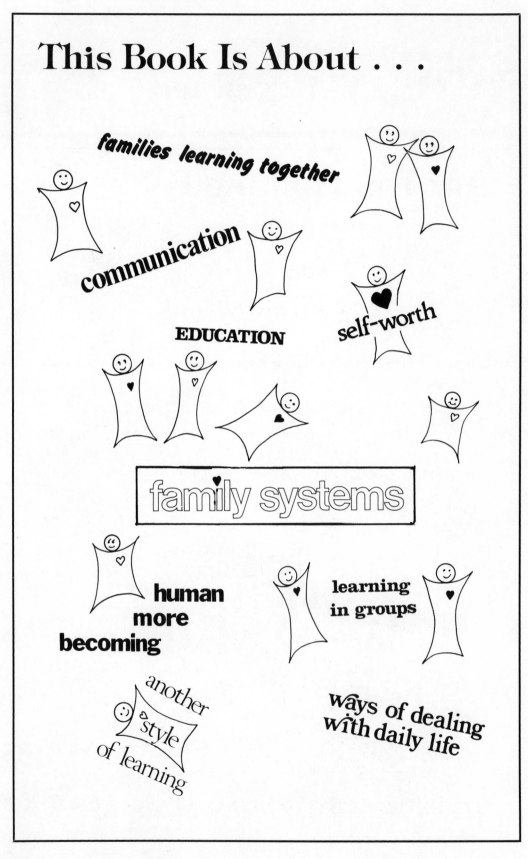

families learning together

communication

EDUCATION

self-worth

family systems

human
more
becoming

learning
in groups

another
style
of learning

ways of dealing
with daily life

In This Book
FAMILY Is Defined . . .

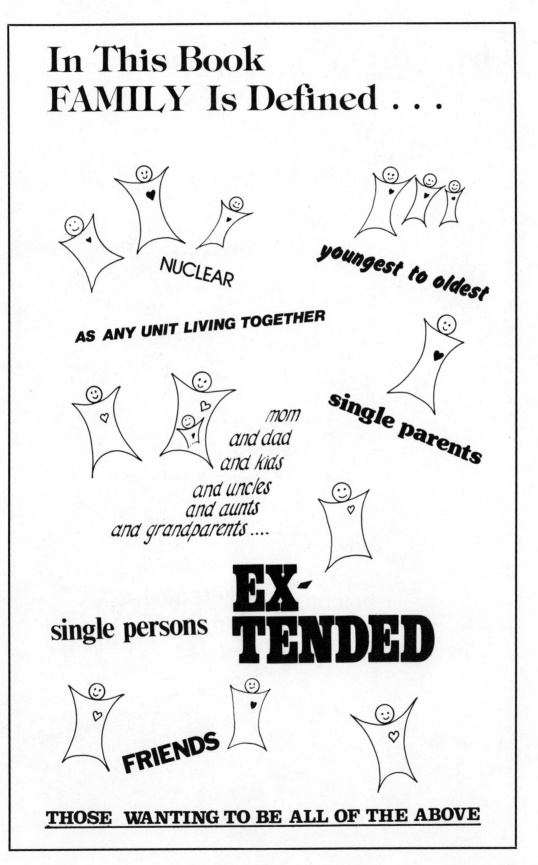

NUCLEAR

youngest to oldest

AS ANY UNIT LIVING TOGETHER

single parents

mom
and dad
and kids
and uncles
and aunts
and grandparents ....

single persons **EX-TENDED**

FRIENDS

THOSE WANTING TO BE ALL OF THE ABOVE

Do You Wonder About . . .

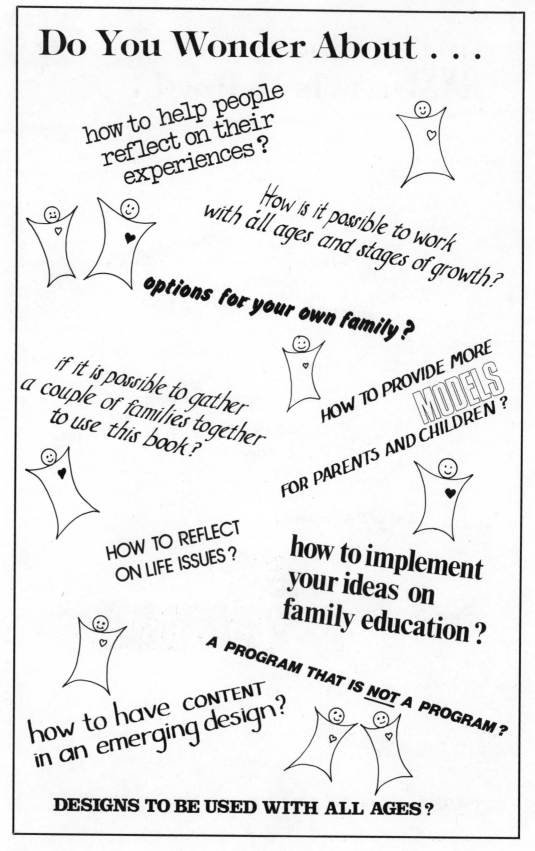

how to help people reflect on their experiences?

How is it possible to work with all ages and stages of growth?

options for your own family?

if it is possible to gather a couple of families together to use this book?

HOW TO PROVIDE MORE MODELS FOR PARENTS AND CHILDREN?

HOW TO REFLECT ON LIFE ISSUES?

how to implement your ideas on family education?

A PROGRAM THAT IS NOT A PROGRAM?

how to have CONTENT in an emerging design?

DESIGNS TO BE USED WITH ALL AGES?

CHAPTER 2

Images

What does multi-family, inter-generational education look like? If you were an observer for an evening, first you would see a large room that shows signs of being prepared with care. It is a room ready for something to happen: around the walls are several posters with questions and incomplete phrases waiting to be completed; in one corner are toys ready to be played with; a large carpet in the center is surrounded by big soft pillows and some comfortable chairs; a perking coffee pot and pitchers of punch are on one table; across the room on a matching table are piles of supplies. The leaders have provided a setting that speaks of involvement, comfort, and caring.

People begin arriving. The first family has a picnic basket, the next comes with each member carrying a brown bag supper, another carries fried chicken boxes. Greetings are called out and are returned with warm smiles. The children go immediately to the posters on the walls and soon call to parents to come and complete the sentences and to see the funny faces they have drawn. Soon the room is alive with activity, happy exchanges, and anticipation of good things to come. The twenty-six people fill the room with hope and an eagerness to begin.

As soon as the last family arrives and has had time to join the others, everyone gathers for the evening meal. After supper the plans for the evening are unveiled, and the people are involved in a variety of activities. During the evening there is . . .

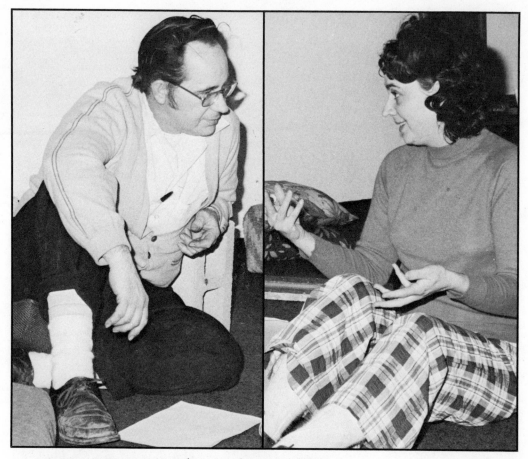

... a time to strengthen relationships

... a time for trusting ... and testing

16

. . . a time to make new friends

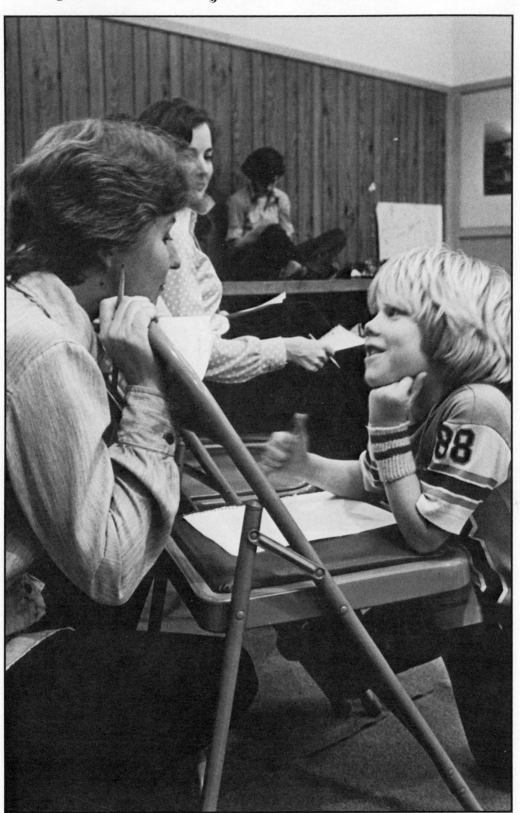

. . . a time for sharing food and fellowship

18

. . . a time for new discoveries in a family

. . . a time for young and old to share

. . . a time to enjoy each other's presence

CHAPTER 3

Stories

Only recently we have come to see inter-generational, multi-family education as a separate, unique discipline. Yet both of us can see in our lives strands of experience that tell us that inter-generational education has been a part of our lives from the beginning. As we have worked together, bits and pieces of our stories have been shared with each other, along with certain values we hold important and certain questions we ponder about the way people learn. We would like to tell you our stories—what has brought us to a belief in multi-family education and to the development of a particular model. Together our stories will help to put into context all that follows. Our pathways have been marked by searching, reflecting, sharing, and changing. As we look back, we see that the pieces fit as part of the process. The pathway and the pieces are parts of our model. As you read, as you recall your story and reflect on your life and the processes at work in it, we are guessing that you will touch base with us along the way.

Jack's Story

For the first ten years of my life I lived with my family in a small village in eastern Oregon. Much of our life in that village was inter-generational and multi-family with major gatherings at the schoolhouse (which was really a community center). I remember programs, picnics, dances, and celebrations when the whole town gathered. I remember happy times listening to stories told by older members and looking at pictures of days gone by. The village was too small for a church, but we occasionally had Sunday School, and I do remember the town gathering for prayer at times of crises.

I lived in a family where it was okay to try new things—to paint, draw, garden, sew, build—and if someone was not available to help when we reached a difficult spot, we were encouraged to search for the answer or for the help that was needed. The results of our explorations were shared with the larger family and with friends. It was okay to ask questions, and we were given time to explore the answers.

I looked forward to the times when cousins, aunts, and uncles would come to visit. With only a little encouragement from us young 'uns, stories of the "good old days" were told—sometimes with laughter and sometimes in solemn tones. A lot of my "growing up" time was spent with grandparents. I recall the stories that were shared: my grandfather's journey from Norway and my grandmother's coming West in a covered wagon. The natural, normal, and good life was inter-generational.

We sometimes thought the rules were strict, but they were clear. There were certain things the Hilyard kids could and could not do. The village was small, so that word got back home if we tried something that wasn't approved.

When we left the village and moved to town, we all wondered what this change would mean. We found our sense of community continuing in two places. Family never meant just my immediate family; it continued to mean cousins, aunts, uncles, grandparents, and sometimes friends. Our home was often the gathering place to share celebrations of joy and sorrow. The larger community was found in church as we took our place in the worship and in other activities there.

The greatest shock in moving to town was school. We had been in a one room school with six grades and a system of interdependence, but now we were separated and felt competitive with our classmates. Yet gradually, after I learned the ways of dealing with the new system, I began to enjoy school.

I liked learning and, in fact, I enjoyed all activities throughout junior and senior high school. Experiences in these early activities helped to shape a vocational choice and led me to a double major in art and education. Art helped me to explore a talent; education helped me to discover processes of learning and to reflect on life. During college years my journey in my own faith followed what I now see as a typical path—one of testing and exploring—from belief to unbelief to belief and faith. And it wasn't only intellectual, or "head-tripping"—a community of Episcopal college students took me in and experientially we shared a faith.

Following college my first job was teaching art and drama in a high school and supervising an art program in several elementary schools. My own family was changed by my marriage to Jane, and we shared teaching in the same school system. Those years were fun. My hope for my classes—both art and drama—was that through the art forms the students would be able to express who they were and give shape to their hopes and dreams. The plays we chose were plays that explored life. I still have some drawings from those first teaching years and carry good memories.

Still, as good as those years were, something was missing. Lives were not changed by school alone, and kids followed the same unfulfilling patterns of parents. That missing link led me to the seminary. In my reflection I thought that surely there must be a way (other than formal classrooms with desks in rows) to share the truth and joy of life.

There are two things that stand out about life in the seminary. First, my most significant learnings about life and faith came from the community itself as we shared joys and sorrows; and the books we studied gave us a language to describe what was happening to us. The second was a fascination with religious education. The Episcopal church was developing what was known as the Seabury Series, a life-centered curriculum. It was exciting to prepare lessons, to listen for the questions, and to find similar questions and responses in our heritage and faith.

After ordination I was given what many young assistants are given: the youth group and the church school. I recall the tensions between passing along information and dealing with the real questions. Parents and teachers asked for help in passing on information about Bible, the creeds, liturgy, and church history. Too often this was merely information which had nothing to do with a living faith.

After I spent several years in parish ministry, another opportunity came along: some training in human relations in a laboratory setting. These two weeks in my life stand out as high points. They were important to me because I gained both a new understanding of myself and an insight into the dynamics at work in group life. Never before had I experienced the power available to a group as it took charge of its own life. The experiences were powerful enough to help me change my style of relating to people and to give me an understanding of design in working with the real questions people asked.

Ten years were spent in campus ministry during those "turbulent times." It was there that the sense of interdependence was deepened within me, an interdependence that went far beyond the group to a vision of world-wide interdependence and interrelatedness. However, as hours of counseling added up in my working with students and parents toward bridging a gap in communication and differing values, I became more aware of areas of conflict between parent and child. Our home was open while all of this was happening, providing a place where students could come and talk. With my own children entering into the conversation and sharing, there were always several generations present.

My children have helped me to see one other facet of our life that has been important. We have in our diocese an annual clergy family camp—a week on the Oregon coast where we live, talk, sing, worship, play, and study together as one large, extended family. My children fondly recall these weeks as very special times—times in which they have a sense of freedom in a caring community that they find nowhere else.

While we were in Michigan (the last three years of college chaplaincy ministry), my children missed the clergy camp experience. I was invited to help staff a communicating arts conference; while the staff was planning, I realized this might be the experience my children missed. I invited them to join me. This was an inter-generational, multi-family experience using various art forms to build community. It was a good week as we shared what we made with our hands and hearts, as we shared dreams and visions. Later it was my children who encouraged me to try this model again, and they were the chief recruiters.

Two weeks after returning to Oregon as director of Christian Education for the diocese, I found that the education department and a local Roman Catholic community were sponsoring a family camp. I had never been to one, and I decided that I should attend. Thus, while the family stayed home to unpack boxes, I went to a "fantasy family camp." Jeanette Benson and I were assigned to the same group. As we lived in the fantasy of Trina Paulus' *Hope for the Flowers*, experiencing the theology woven into the story and learning from the three-year-old who was part of our group as well as from the adults, we discovered "family education."

That experience did two things for me. The use of the "children's" story brought me back to the collection of children's books that my wife and I have shared—rereading for the simple but profound truths that are woven into and underneath the stories. The experience also began to guide my reading as I was getting back into religious education. Almost every journal and magazine had some article on family education, and I began to devour them all. One name surfaced with many references to a book with an intriguing title—Virginia Satir and her book, *Peoplemaking*. She wrote what I believed, and her book has become "the Bible" of my family education. Another name surfaced with a model: the name was Margaret Sawin, and the model was called Family Clustering. Jane and I were invited to become part of the staff of an experimental training lab in family education where Margaret was the resource person. It was during that week that I discovered that much of what I had already been doing in my work was family education and that many of my beliefs were based on its principles.

In the next few months Jeanette and I were often at the same conferences, and when we had time to chat it was most often about discoveries and beliefs in family education. When a phone call came from her one day suggesting the possibility of our writing a book, I could only say, "Sure, when?"

Jeanette's Story

My journey along paths that led to the one I am now traveling, *family education*, began long before I was aware of paths, journeys, and goals.

My models were my parents—in questing, trusting hunches, and risking for what seemed to fit for their lives. I was born on a small island in Alaska where my inter-generational, non-traditional education began. This process was rarely interrupted by traditional schooling. There was the very special time when I lived on another island in a lighthouse! The school on that island was the "one room schoolhouse" where most grades had only one pupil and where we were taught many subjects together. Challenges and modeling came from adults and the "big kids." Programs for holidays were grand events with adults and children learning together rather than giving performances. From here my education continued in a school without walls, the Pribilof Islands in the Bering Sea. In retrospect, those were my richest learning years. I learned experientially; the content was life at the moment, and I was surrounded by adult models of various ages and stages in their development. It was during these years, I now realize, that I discovered the freedom to learn, to "go outside the lines," and to reflect and come away with a new awareness. This process was modeled and encouraged by my parents and other adults.

My education in traditional schools was exciting for me because it was another new learning experience. Not having come through the system, I had huge gaps in my knowledge according to traditional norms and standards. In my experiences in dealing with this I discovered that when a need arose I could easily learn what was necessary. This process also proved true in areas of enrichment to which I had not previously been exposed.

However, after two years of college, I took a quantum leap into tradition, structure, and systematized learning and educating. At this point I was aware of the modeling of my teachers and friends. The joy and freedom of a life style so opposite mine attracted me to the point of deciding to enter a religious community, the Sisters of Providence, Seattle Province. My continued experiences and learnings from dealing with likenesses, differences, tensions, challenges, and resolutions from this (now not so structured) new life style raised some of the key issues in my quest for a humanizing educational process.

Then when I became a teacher as a nun in the Catholic school system, I began my search for a meaningful religious education. Except for my last three years of high school and college, I had not been in that system; thus, for a good part of my search, I thought what I was seeking was what I had missed in my education. I discovered years later that what I was looking for in my own learning and in that of my students hadn't been in the system generally. I was looking for something before and beyond the rote catechism, something that spoke to life here and now. In that search I traveled down many an exciting path of fine

24

religious education programs—programs that were taking giant steps in understanding faith, how it is shared and learned, what that process is about, and what human growth and development mean in education.

I began my degree work in religious education, soon became acquainted with every religion program that came off the press, and piloted many of them. For my degree thesis I wrote my own program, the result of my own course for first graders. I later found it highly successful with eighth graders, with the main adaptation being necessary with the material that related to life experiences.

In my search I moved into the teaching of high school religion and discovered very soon the need for models. I helped design a weekend retreat program that brought together adults and teenagers for the purpose of sharing together a lived faith. It seemed to me that there were not enough adult models. I moved to adult education in parish work. Now I see the process—of searching and trying out many an adult education program, and going to workshops to learn what I had missed—was repeated. I discovered in time that the best programs were those designed for the life experiences of a particular group, those programs that *continually emerged* to meet the needs and faith experiences of the group members.

It was while I was on this path that I met Dr. Margaret Sawin, who began the Family Cluster model in Rochester, New York. I had met her first in my readings, and then I discovered that she was to be at a convention in Chicago in November of 1973. I went to this meeting and attended her session. There I was affirmed in the path I was taking and in the programs I was designing. I gained confidence and further direction along the road clearly marked *family education*. It was early on this path that I met Virginia Satir, who has been a singular inspiration, guide, and model for me in my journey toward religious education (based not only upon the Gospel value system but also upon the model of Jesus, the Teacher).

I am now *doing* what I have been so long searching for—basic religious education. My focus is a human growth and development model. I see the model to be the foundation for the expression of a dynamic faith-life. What follows in this book does not belong to any one body of religious beliefs; what is here belongs to all persons at all times, preceding and transcending a belief system. This book speaks of belief in each person, his/her value, his/her orientation toward good, his/her need to be in relationships, his/her freedom to choose and to become.

Jack and I met when both of us were solidly on the family education route. It was at a family camp which had for its purpose linking people of all ages in exploring a particular value through fantasy literature. Since that meeting we have worked together in many ways. I have been challenged, encouraged, and supported by Jack at various turns and blocks along the way to this moment— when we are giving you our mutual support and encouragement to explore our path of family education.

Together, we urge you to dedication in your explorations and discoveries as you join us to make more accessible the way of multi-family, multi-age education.

We have discovered parallel journeys in the events of our lives, in wrestling with questions and values. The outcome is a model of multi-family, inter-generational education. Certain assumptions emerge which have roots in our lives and are expressed in the model.

- Every person has God-given gifts, talents, and skills. We may know them only as they are affirmed, sharpened, integrated, and valued by the community.
- We learn from others in the community—especially through the modeling they provide.
- Reflection on shared experience integrates new learning.
- The experience of every person—from the youngest to the oldest—is valid and is to be honored.
- Learning to cope with change and to integrate it in our lives brings the possibility of growth.
- Learning is facilitated when dealing with real concerns, real situations, and real issues.
- Faith is a living reality shared in the community.

We do not claim that our model is better than all others; we only say that it is a result of where we have been. It is our hope that it may fit with your journey also. Rather than suggesting that you approach it as the latest new model on the market, we would hope that you join us in the process of sharing, reflecting, and changing—bringing your own insights, creativity, and gifts.

CHAPTER 4

Comments

We have shared our stories. Those who have participated in multi-family education sessions also have something to say. The following are direct quotes from responses to a questionnaire sent to a sampling of participants.

"I think family education is a worthwhile experience for every family. I didn't realize how much fun it is to work with my family. It brought us closer together."

Carolyn (age 13)

"When 12- and 16-year-old boys prepare dinner and hurry everyone out of the house to be on time, it has to have a lot to offer. When I hear them telling their friends how neat it was, I know it was a success."

Virginia

"The meeting at which my husband revealed he would sell our business and take me traveling for a year (if we only had one year left together) was worth more than I can say. Family education reinforced all the positive things about our marriage."

Jeanie

"Family education fulfilled a need to relate to others on a personal rather than a social basis and still offers the opportunity to become involved in a group with meaningful objectives and experiences."

Jack

"Family education enabled our family to see ourselves as a family and individuals within a family, through our eyes and observations of others."

Sharon

"I experienced a special constructive time. A family of families in an open atmosphere where roles and ways of communicating were discovered. I learned more about myself and thus I was able to grow."

Dave

"I had fun with my family at family education evenings."

Terry (age 8)

"It (family education) makes you feel important. Everyone is valued the same. It gives you new and different insights."

Julie (age 16)

"Family education offers each member of the family a time, space and process to discover their own 'familiness,' strengthen it and celebrate it."

Barbara

Mary Nell, age 4, dictated the following answer to the question, "If you were going to tell a friend about family education what would you say?"

"Bring your whole family and share singing and fooling around with my family."

"The simple exercises that improved communication within our family structure have been extremely helpful and fun! Of special benefit have been the exercises that allowed us to express our own personal feelings to the other members of our family. I think exercises like this are neat because it is often times so very hard to tell someone—even within your own family—how you feel about a situation or about them. Thanks so much."

Dan (age 17)

"The things we did and made, i.e., masks, painting, mobiles, etc., were very effective and brought out insights which I will not only remember, but which I can put into practice to make me a better person."

Bob

This is just a sample of the responses, and everyone is saying that the experiences were worth the time and effort and that they resulted in growth for themselves individually and as a family. The most effective advertising is done by family members who share with their peer groups their positive feelings about their family education experience.

II Organizing

CHAPTER 5

Using This Book

This book has been designed primarily as a resource book for leaders of intergenerational education groups. By adapting and adding to the designs presented here, a leadership team should have enough designs for a beginning group meeting for ten or twelve weeks, and a good start on an advanced group.

However, there are other ways the book may be used. A single family could use some of the exercises at home. The family might agree to set aside some time each week for several weeks as "family time." Choosing appropriate exercises, the members of the family could select certain areas in which they would like to grow, or certain issues in their lives to which they would like to give attention. Reflecting on actions, interactions, and feelings could provide opportunities for greater understanding and growth.

Several families might agree to meet together to work through some common issues in their lives. When several families work together, there is an opportunity to share values and insights on mutual problem areas, and this facilitates change. There is also greater opportunity to see a variety of styles and solutions. The leadership role might rotate among the members, or the families could contract with an outside leader.

The book could serve as a resource book for religious education programs in local churches—especially for family nights, family weekends, or family camps.

The book is meant to be a starting point—open to wherever the leadership wants to take it. It is our hope that the creative spirit will gradually unfold within the family.

CHAPTER 6

Leading & Facilitating

A basic part of our model is the concept of shared leadership: a complete sharing of the planning, directing, and evaluating by two or three persons. Once you are underway there is no "chief" or "head honcho." The two or three persons make up the leadership team for a multi-family group of about twenty-five persons. If you have caught the vision of family education through inter-generational groups, if it's your task to build a team, if you are "it"—this chapter may have some hints and clues that would be helpful for you. Putting together a team and growing with it can be an exciting experience. With new beginnings there is a sense of adventure. In deciding on guides to present in this chapter, we have taken from our experience those that have proven helpful to us in developing leadership.

If it is your task to find a team of facilitators, look for some people you would like to work with; look for someone who believes in "family" and can see the possibility of education through and with the family. It is helpful if the team members have training in group work (group process or human relations training).

If that is not possible, look for one person who has worked with children: a teacher, a volunteer who is good with Brownie or Cub Scout groups, a mother or dad who likes children. Look for another person who is working with small groups of adults. If you have had experience in family groups, think back to those groups. Often leaders emerge from the groups.

If some skills are lacking, one can always arrange for some in-service training along the way. However, it is a good idea to build this into the leadership agreement at the beginning of the year. We have often established or developed teams for a year and then planned several in-service training events along the way.

It takes time and energy and care to build a team. Trust and openness are two qualities characterizing good team work; there's no magic formula for these qualities. They grow as the team grows to appreciate and honor the gifts each member has to bring.

Once the team is chosen, schedule an afternoon or evening together since there is a need for getting acquainted with one another and with the dynamics of working together. Being open in sharing one's personal investment in the experience as well as hopes for the group will do much toward building trust. Four areas of concern need to be discussed. By agreeing on a few questions in each area and coming to this initial meeting prepared to share responses, the members will be on the way toward becoming a team.

1) *Personal needs and strengths:*

Why do I want to be involved in this experience?

What do I hope to gain from other members of the leadership team?

What do I hope to gain from the total family group?

What special skills and talents do I bring?

What do I hope to learn?

What skills do I want to sharpen?

What are some of the topics in which I could offer expertise?

2) *Hopes for this group experience:*

What are my hopes and dreams for this group?

What is the best thing that could happen to this group?

What is the worst thing that could happen to this group?

What changes might the people in this group make?

3) *Leading and facilitating:*

What am I like as a leader in a group?

How do I share insights and observations?

How do I think people learn in groups?

How do I plan for group experiences?

4) *Family education theory:*

What is my approach to family education?

How can families learn from one another?

What do I hope the exercises will provide for families?

This initial meeting is the key to building a team. The option to renegotiate should be left open to facilitate adding a member (if you feel some necessary skills are missing) or allowing a member to drop out (if working styles or beliefs about learning are too diverse for comfort).

Once the team is set, it is a good idea to get out calendars and to block out times for planning for the whole period. In the beginning weeks you may need a three-hour block of time each week; later on you may decide to adjust the time allotment. (See chapter 7 on Planning for more details.) Take a look at the personal needs of the team. Some team members need more time, some need to share the personal joys and frustrations in life along the way, some need time to think alone, and others are quite content to do just the task at hand.

In addition to the actual planning session, there are other blocks of time that are important to the life of the team.

Before Each Session

In addition to preparing the room and arranging the supplies, plan to spend a few minutes checking where you are as persons. Are there pressures or joys to share? Has anything been happening in your life that would indicate changing some of the responsibilities in the plan for the evening? The schedule is never carved in stone; shared planning facilitates the shifting of responsibilities.

After Each Session

The leadership team should plan some debriefing at the end of the group session, checking each other's feelings, perceptions, and insights regarding the session.

• How did the session go? (A rating scale might be helpful.)

• How did you fulfill the purpose?

• Are any group members hurting?

• Did some "lights" go on?

• What observations about the group need to be shared?

• What observations about the leadership need to be shared?

• What changes might you want to make in the design?

• What ideas might be suggested for the next step?

32

It is a good idea to begin to think about the next step so each team member can do some homework. With the data from the evening fresh in one's mind, establishing the direction for the next session is easy to do. Then, after some work and thinking at home, the next planning session goes much more smoothly.

We have learned some things about building teams—some of them the hard way. It is helpful if families of the leadership team have had some inter-generational group experiences. When one is just beginning a program that may not be possible, but if the families have had some group experience they can offer help to a parent who is a leader, because they know something of what the experience entails. The family members will have an understanding of the kind of time involved and will realize that not all of the experience of the family program can be shared. We have also found that it is best to schedule husbands and wives in three-member teams. In addition, it is wise not to have family members in the same group where parents are leaders; it is difficult to be both an objective leader and a sharing participant.

Family group members learn from experience and from each other; they also learn from the modeling of the leadership team. From the earliest sessions of a family group it is important for the leadership team members to model "feeling statements" and "I statements" and to make the statements free of judgments. Most people have little experience in expressing their own feelings, especially in group situations. Often those who do talk about their feelings will begin, "I *think* we feel . . .," confusing thinking with feeling and offering their opinions for the whole group.

Modeling by the leaders may show participants a new way of behaving or a new way of looking at a situation. Modeling also frees the participants and gives an "OK" to the new behavior. The participants will watch the communication style and the group interaction of the team.

CHAPTER 7

Planning

The planning cycle:
data
purpose
plan
evaluation

We work with the concept of *emerging* design; the content flows out of the group and the data. We may have a general direction in mind when we begin and may know what we hope to cover over the several weeks the group is to be together. However, the life of the group and what happens with the members of the group may rearrange the parts or may totally change the direction as new questions emerge or as the level of comprehension varies. The planning cycle is our guide for our work, week by week.

Data   That collection of all the pieces of information you have about the participants is part of the data. One begins to look for significant actions, comments, and questions. Other pieces of data are collected through evaluations, however formal or informal they may be, as well as through other collectors. (See chapter 9 on Data Collecting.)

Through the home interview you will gather data about the hopes and expectations of the participants. You will observe how the family system operates, noting who makes the decisions and who speaks for whom. You may want some additional information from the participants which can be collected by means of a written form. From week to week you will have data from the group activities and from verbal or written evaluations.

Take a look at the data and arrange the pieces to offer you some useful information. If it comes on written forms, collate each question and comment. It is helpful to list the responses on newsprint. If the data is information from observations or from notes, arrange the bits and pieces in categories that will help to focus on priorities. *The data needs to be organized for meaningful use.*

As a team, ask yourselves the following questions as you explore the data:
• What are the common threads?
• What are the needs being expressed?
• What are the expectations being expressed?
• What do the participants want to learn?
• What do they want to do?
• How many people want this?

Once you have organized and discussed the data and have found the common threads you are ready to move on.

Purpose   Use the data to develop a purpose statement. This is a short, concise statement of your goals or intentions for the next session. The following is a good check list to test your purpose statement:

- Is it based on the data?
- Is it a short, sharply focused intention?
- Is it realistic? Can it be accomplished?
- Is it measurable? Can the results be checked?

It takes time to write a purpose statement, but the time is well spent. The purpose helps to determine all that follows. When the leadership team agrees on a statement of purpose, a direction is set for planning.

Plan

The plan or procedure is the design for an evening's session. You will want to use exercises that will help the participants discover, explore, practice, and learn. Aim for reality. Keep the plan simple. Stay within the capabilities of the participants. Determine whether the design can be accomplished within the time allowed. As you look for exercises or design new ones, ask yourselves, "Will they help to accomplish the purpose?"

Evaluation

In the plan for each evening's session allow some time for the participants to respond to the activities. You may design a simple written form with questions, such as:
- What did you learn?
- What did you like best?
- What did you like least?
- What was the most important discovery you made tonight?

Or you may use the general reflection time to gather some verbal reactions. These responses and reactions are part of the data needed for the planning cycle to begin again.

This cycle becomes a way of life. It is a supporting structure which allows the group life to determine the course and direction for the educational experience.

In our work together we have also discovered four blocks of time that are part of the planning process:
- Debriefing time
- Homework time
- Team planning time
- Pre-session check-in time

The few minutes immediately following a session are important for debriefing. Take the time to share feelings and reactions. During this time make some notes about possibilities for the next session. What does the data say? Agree to think about and do research on particular areas.

You have your homework. What are some exercises, games, stories you might suggest? As good ideas often come at odd moments, be ready for them. Schedule this block early enough to get the job done and not so close to the family group meetings that you are under pressure.

Make good use of the team planning time. You may want to agree on a given length of time. Review the data from the last session in the light of the overall movement of the educational experience. Your first task is to arrive at a purpose. Once this is done, look for and design activities that will help achieve that purpose. If the exercise is new, try it out and practice giving directions. Decide who is going to do each part and who is going to observe. It is often helpful as a means of growing if one of the team members observes what you are working on. Ask yourself, "What can I learn?" or "What do I need?" If you want to check on how your direction-giving comes across, ask a team member to observe and to share his or her evaluation of how well you did. The family group is an opportunity for you to grow also. If you ask, you will get some reactions to what you did and how well you did it. If you did a good job, the "strokes" are nice to receive; if you want to grow, it is good to get those hints and helps from a friend and teammate.

During the pre-session check-in time you can make last minute changes. Since a few days have passed since planning time, supplies, directions, and arrangements should be carefully checked.

You are ready to go. Have a good session!

CHAPTER 8

Contracting

It takes much re-scheduling and rearranging of time for families to agree to come together with other families every week for ten or twelve weeks. It is even a considerable challenge for a single family to free a night when all members can be present each week. Each family and each member in the family is committing some prime time to the family education experience. Thus, it is important that this time be *contracted for* in several ways.

As clear as your advertising might be, there will still be as many concepts about what is going to happen during family education sessions as there are people agreeing to come. For this reason it is essential for the leadership to go to the home of each family to contract with the family as a *whole* for the family series. Our experience has borne out very consistently that any family who has unclear concepts, expectations, and commitments about the sessions is a family who, for a variety of reasons, usually the press of time, was not visited and contracted in the home by the leaders. Our process has been the following:

• After registration and formation of the group, each family is notified of their acceptance and of the night they will have their sessions. Use this mailing as another opportunity to educate toward another model. That is, rather than "We are happy to inform you . . .," try something similar to the following:

Home Contracts

Good News—Happy Days

_____(list all family members)_____

will be in Family Education on _____ evenings. You will receive a call from a team leader to set up a convenient time to visit you in your home, to meet the whole family, and to respond to any questions you may have.

WELCOME!

Signed _____

• Team leaders who are going to lead that particular series will call each family and schedule the visits. It is important that every family member will be available that evening, early enough so that the youngest will be there.

• During the visit begin data gathering. Note carefully what *names* or *nicknames* they prefer. Note the maturity level of the children (older six, young ten, etc.); attitude of teenagers; relationships, including authority structure; psychological space; freedom to speak what is felt, heard, or seen.

• Encourage family members to share expectations, fears, hopes, doubts, and just plain wonderings.

• Home agreements should be read, discussed, and signed.

The home visit provides for the family a relaxed atmosphere on the family's turf to get to know the leaders while getting information and assurance that will make a significant difference in freedom and openness even in the first session.

Following are two samples of agreements signed during the home visit. We recommend the families put it on the kitchen bulletin board as a continual reminder during the series.

FAMILY EDUCATION AGREEMENT

Family Education is a time of learning and fun. Some activities will be done within your family, others with different groups of people. Each person will have an opportunity to talk and reflect about ways of communicating, about sharing responsibility, and about the role of rules and self-worth within the family. It is an opportunity for all to learn in a relaxed and fun atmosphere.

Family Education is held during the dinner hour. Sharing a meal together will be an important community-building exercise during the series. Community will be one of our aims. Supper will be a brown bag affair. Each family will bring their own; coffee and Kool-aid will be provided.

Yes, I agree to keep (day)_____ evenings from (date)_____ to (date)_____ free for Family Education.
I will be present at 5:30 and remain until 7:30.
In case of illness or emergency for anyone in the family, someone will call (phone no.)_____ .

Signed (family members): _____

Leaders: _____

THE _____ FAMILY'S CONTRACT

FOR FAMILY EDUCATION

There are several assumptions which form the basis for the family education model. These assumptions will become experience during the ten-week Family Education Series.

The assumptions are:

a) God has made every individual a person of unique worth and has given him or her amazing gifts.

b) Self-worth and personal awareness are best realized in a supportive community where each person is committed to the other persons in the group.

c) A certain amount of self-disclosure or history-giving is necessary before the supportive community can enable each person to give.

d) The way to call forth the best in each other is to affirm each other's strengths.

e) The spiritual dimension must be realized in the process of enabling a person to discover his or her fuller self-hood.

f) Celebration is the natural result when love, trust, and acceptance are expressed by a community of people committed to one another.

I agree to:

Be present every (day)_____ for the next ten weeks.

Be on time (actual time)_____.

Remain until (actual time)_____.

Call (phone no.)_____ in case of illness or emergency.

FAMILY MEMBERS   LEADERS

_____   _____

_____   _____

_____   _____

_____   _____

CHAPTER 9

Data Collecting & Evaluation

Data Collecting

Family education events, in order to make change and growth possible for the family members, deal with the here and now in design. As was stated in the chapter entitled "Using This Book," our designs are not part of a packaged program but ideas to spark your own ingenuity and creativity so that you are enabled to use best what is happening in the here and now with your group of families. The designs are not to be unwrapped each week, but they are to emerge from the data collected during previous sessions, such as unanswered questions, the level of trust and comfort, and the freedom to share ideas and feelings.

In addition to the data gathered during the home visit you may want some further information with which to build the first evening. We send out "data collectors" to gather needed information for this purpose. The following is a compilation of several data collectors used over a period of years. It is offered here as a springboard for you to design your own gathering of the initial information you need to begin your event. It is important to keep in mind that this information, even though helpful, has limitations. It is only a part (and a very small part) of the data you gather over the ten weeks.

Some Suggested Questions for a Written Data Collector

What do you have the most fun doing with your family?
What do you like about your family?
What is the happiest part of your day?
When you have good news to share, with whom do you share it first?
  In my family I like to tell first _____
  Why do you say this?
I hope my family will _____
My special free-time activities are _____
Two neat things about my family are _____
The ways in which I like to learn are _____
Do you have a musical instrument or a talent that you would be willing to bring and share with the group? If so, what is it? _____

Older persons can be secretaries for younger ones; younger ones can often answer by using an illustration.

Gathering data is a continual process and as such is one of the key tasks of leadership. Listening with an "inner ear" to the responses and the interactions provides material for the next step(s) in your design. Read any notes or preliminary plans you have made in light of new data from the previous session and from data you gathered from the home visits with each family.

Evaluation

In order that this data collection does not become a list of assumptions instead

40

of reasonably accurate feedback, there should be a "check-out" time at the end of each session. This time of evaluation, temperature-reading, and opportunity for direct input from participants is vital if needs are going to be met and the sessions are to deal with real concerns and issues in the families. There are many ways of facilitating this. One way is through modeling by sharing your feelings about what is happening and about what you are learning about self in the various interactions. Sometimes some definite questions are helpful: "What has been most helpful to you?" "How do you feel about what just happened in your family, or in the group?" "Would someone like to share a new learning from this experience?"

Another method we often use is the temperature-reading, an idea of Virginia Satir. Temperature-taking relates to what *Bugs* you about what has happened or is happening, to *Willies* (the questions and anxieties that you have about what has happened or is happening), to *Pricklies* (what you don't feel good about), and to *Warm Fuzzies* (what you feel really good about).

Any one of these opens the way for people to share where they are and to give suggestions. *All* persons, youngest as well as oldest, should be encouraged to state their feelings and to ask questions. Evaluation or data gathering time provides an opportunity for leaders to ask questions to clarify their data and to check out information and assumptions.

A week represents a lot of living; each person and each family will come the following week with a new set of experiences, psychological spaces, and feelings. It is important, therefore, to take time for a temperature-reading at the beginning of the evening to get everyone on board again as well as to gather live data. This data supplies information enabling you, the leader, to re-check your design for necessary adjustment, realignment, or modification. There could also be circumstances of death, birth, job loss, or sudden move that may require changing your whole plan. This should be done with the consensus of the group after the alternate plan has been shared and clarified.

The more you gather and respond to data, the more comfortable the group will be, and the more here and now issues will be raised from individuals and family units. When this is happening, the time spent in planning and in working with the group will become increasingly more effective. Data collecting and evaluating will have then become one step in your group process.

CHAPTER 10

Space & Arrangement & Materials

Physical space is an important factor in every activity in this book, whether the activity is done as a single family unit or as a group of families. There should be enough space for individuals to work by themselves as well as space to do freely whatever movement is asked for. There should be enough space for families to be together comfortably. It should be an area that is not harmed by occasional spills of paint, glue, and similar materials.

There should be a large, comfortable, warm room with restrooms close by. If several families come together, it is helpful to find a place in a church that could be neutral ground, so that the families with sufficient space in their homes aren't always hosting. Indoor/outdoor carpeting is comfortable and can take a lot of Kool-aid, glue, and paint. Old soft furniture, lots of pillows, a beanbag chair or two, and at least one large table for supplies and some working surface combine to make a *family education room*.

We usually have a "play corner" in our family education room. This is a designated area with creative toys, blocks, Tinker Toys, etc., for younger children to use when they have the need. Our experience is that children move in and out of this area very freely and that even in the play area they are a vital part of the whole group.

If your group decides to begin by eating a meal together, you may want a large enough table for all to gather around. Another option that we often use is to sit on the floor, eating picnic style. For this purpose we use low tables made of cement blocks and boards covered with contact paper. These serve us well for meals and are also useful for writing and working space.

It will be evident that some type of storage space for materials and projects is a necessity. Space is easier to come by than actual storage cupboards; but, in any event, decisions will have to be made regarding the storage and transportation of materials. As you read the list of suggested materials and see what is needed for any activity, you will see that you can save both time and money by having the materials on hand. Another kind of space that is important is *wall space*—sometimes for display purposes and sometimes for work areas.

In the years we have used this model of family education we have worked in an interesting variety of spaces and all have had limitations (some more than others), but all have been workable. If you know the ideal, you will be better able to work creatively with the reality you face.

Materials/ Equipment

Most of the materials, you will notice, have been recycled. What needs to be gathered or purchased is:
• Large roll of butcher paper

42

- Newsprint (there will be times when you will need the weight of butcher paper, but many times newsprint would serve as well)
- Felt pens or markers in many colors
- Large container of crayons (these need not be new)
- Small bottles of glue (and a large one from which to refill)
- Scissors (several with blunt points for younger people)

The following are great to have and may be gathered by the participants during the series:
- Dress-up clothes and costumes
- A variety of scraps of paper, cardboard (often a print shop will give these away rather than throw them away)
- Yarn (all kinds)
- A collection of cottage cheese cartons, paper towel rolls, plastic meat and vegetable containers, TV dinner trays, etc.
- Clay
- Tempera paint and starch for fingerpainting

The list will grow, limited only by your imagination and creativity.

Audio-visual equipment which may be needed at certain times are a record player, an overhead projector, a slide projector, and a movie projector. You could arrange to borrow these as needed; they would not have to be at your disposal every time. An opaque projector, which is fun for a variety of sharings, may be borrowed from a school or church.

CHAPTER 11

Evening Sessions

At this point you may be wondering how a family education evening is scheduled. As the model is one of emerging design, the format and time arrangement are flexible. We think, however, it would be helpful to share with you two rather typical evening schedules. Schedule One includes two shorter activities, and Schedule Two has one longer activity. With the exception of the beginning and ending, time frames are approximate.

Schedule One

5:15-5:30	Stems, checking-in
5:30-6:00	Evening meal
6:00-6:10	Warm up exercises such as a short game or a song, something enjoyable and lively to bring everyone together
6:10-6:30	A short exercise
6:30-6:45	Reflection within simulated family or own family
6:45-7:00	Another short exercise
7:00-7:15	Reflection within a specified group
7:15-7:25	General reflection, evaluation, closure
7:25-7:30	Clean-up, with everyone helping

For both relaxation and transition, it is helpful to sing or to play a short game or do some physical exercise between reflection and a new exercise.

Schedule Two

5:15-5:30	Stems, checking-in
5:30-6:00	Evening meal
6:00-6:10	A game or song with whole group
6:10-6:40	A long exercise
6:40-6:55	Reflection within simulated family
6:55-7:15	Reflection within own family
7:15-7:25	General reflection, evaluation, closure
7:25-7:30	Clean-up, with everyone helping

Again, we would sing or do something brief and active between the long exercise and first reflection and between the two reflections. If your group has several younger children, it is important to provide some physical activity between the working sessions.

III Exercises

CHAPTER 12

Using the Exercise Sheets

All the exercises have been arranged in the same format. They appear in six sections: Introductions, Communication, Self-Worth, Family System, Celebration & Closure, and Transitions. The first five sections are major areas in family and group life; the final section includes a variety of short activities which may serve as warm-up exercises or transitions between other exercises. Each section has a short introduction which includes information for the leadership team.

Each page is labeled in the upper left hand corner with the name of one of the major sections. A few of the exercises might fit another category with some slight changes in directions or reflective questions.

Title Each exercise is given a name. Some are descriptive of the content, while others indicate the launching device or area of learning opportunity.

Aim The purpose or intention of each exercise is stated concisely. This aim will point to the area of concern or learning to be considered.

For The grouping for which the major part of the exercise is intended is given here. Some exercises may include activities for individuals, others for simulated families and actual families. The grouping for which the aim (see above) is intended is usually the one listed here.

Time A time guide for each part of the exercise is indicated. Time may vary with each group. Exercises may take a longer time if the participants get very involved or if new areas for questions are opened. Groups with a number of small children may require more time for activities and less time for reflection. It is more important to pay attention to persons than to pay attention to a rigid time schedule.

Materials The supplies needed to complete the exercise are listed. (See chapter 10 on Space & Arrangement & Materials for a complete listing of the usual kinds of supplies it is helpful to gather and to have available.) In some cases special forms, sets of questions, or sets of directions may be needed. These appear with the exercises. Appropriate amounts should be prepared before the session begins.

Directions The directions have been written for the leader. Each step or change is clearly indicated. It will be necessary for the leader to put the directions in his or her own words. In instances where a series of steps is required, it is helpful if these are printed clearly on newsprint or butcher paper and posted. Some exercises require the directions to be duplicated for each participant or group.

Suggestions for General Reflection These suggestions are meant to serve as a guide for the kind of reflective questions a leader may want to ask the group. Often the questions come out of the group itself; when they do, the leader will want to help the group respond to them. Generally the leader will aim to help the group members clarify and state feelings and to help the members put their learnings or understandings into words. Reflection is a key area and should not be passed over lightly—this is the way new understandings get organized, verbalized, and owned.

Some of the possibilities for variations are suggested. As you work with the exercises you will find other variations.

Variations or Suggestions

All of the exercises have been tried with inter-generational groups. They come from a variety of sources. Some were designed for a particular family education group, some are adapted from exercises used in other training groups, and others were designed especially for this book. The variety offers examples and models for the way new exercises might be developed.

The exercises provide opportunities for learning, changing, and growing. None of them demand, require, or prescribe a particular change. Each person is free to make his or her own choices. The exercises provide an arena where discoveries and choices can be made.

In choosing an exercise the leadership team should ask:
    Does it fit the purpose for this section?
    Does it fit the group?
    Does it fit the concerns being expressed?
    Will it fit our time frame?
    How might it be varied to fit our needs?

After the choices have been made, there are other preparations that are essential:

1) Put the directions in your own words. State them simply and concisely. It is a good idea to practice giving the directions within the team to check for clarity and understanding. If there are a series of steps to an exercise or if there are several questions, it is helpful to post these on newsprint or duplicate a set for each working group.

2) Make a dry run. Go through the several steps in the session plan. This gives each person on the leadership team an opportunity to clarify roles and responsibilities.

3) If the exercise or activity is new, try it with the team. For example, if you have never fingerpainted, it is important to experience fingerpainting before sharing it with the group.

4) Arrange the room and get out the necessary supplies ahead of time. Check to see that the art and craft supplies are usable. Dried up paint or worn out felt pens may ruin a whole plan. If you are using audio-visual equipment, be sure to check it out; a burned-out bulb may throw your whole design.

5) If the exercise requires some sub-grouping, decide how this is to be done. It may be important in some exercises to split family members or to give participants the opportunity to work with and to observe new models. If the participants are not to choose their groups, these can be arranged by the leadership team during planning time.

Other things to keep in mind:

1) *Considering age and development level:* In some of the exercises the very young children will need some help. This is good learning in itself—both the asking for help by the younger children and the offering of help to children other than one's own. If there are several pre-school children, you might choose exercises that don't require writing, or you may vary the exercise to provide pairs in which an older person can be a scribe for a younger child. Some groups feel free to let the younger children play during the discussion time. Some groups may want to develop an atmosphere in which the children are free to come and go around the center of activity. In any case, you may want to provide a play corner with books, toys, games, and puzzles which the children can use freely.

2) *Introducing an exercise:* As a leadership team you will have to decide whether to state the purpose for the session or the aim for the exercise. Some leaders prefer to post these statements, feeling they provide the intention and can be the yardstick for evaluation. Others prefer to use the purpose and aim statements as guidelines for the team. Often these statements can be terribly wordy. If they are shared with the whole group, keep the language simple and clear. Whether you do or don't share them with the group, the point is to describe what you are going to do in such a way as to heighten the interest of the whole group. Where's the fun and where's the excitement in the exercise? This is a clue for introducing it.

3) *Contracting in family groups:* A few of the exercises suggest that the family make a contract in the particular area of concern. If the word contract conveys too harsh and legalistic a sound, use agreement or covenant. Before introducing an exercise that requires contracting, it is important that the leader share the contracting process. One family member begins by stating a request in personal terms. "I need . . .," "I want . . .," "I would like . . .," or "I would hope that . . .," asking for a particular action or change. Other family members respond in personal terms stating what they might offer the situation. "I can do . . .," "I will try . . .," or "I can offer . . ." Some discussion may be necessary to reach consensus. The family then agrees on a time frame for trying the agreed changes (usually a week) and agrees to evaluate the situation at the end of that time with the option to make a new contract.

4) *The use of music:* Singing is very helpful in family education groups. There is bonding that comes with singing together and sharing music. One can often find songs that speak to particular themes or issues. If the suggestions or the talents can come from the group, the use of music is even better. Transitions and closure are often achieved easily through the use of music.

If music is not in the talent bank of the leadership team, talk to a primary teacher for suggestions for action songs. Look in the music section of a good educational bookstore for song books and records. Some guitarists, especially those who play for folk masses, will have suggestions for simple folk songs.

5) *The use of stories:* Some children's stories will provide the basis for developing new exercises or will provide an introduction to an evening session. We have found several authors particularly helpful: Leo Lionni, Brian Hall, Gerald

McDermott, and C. S. Lewis. Other stories and books may be more helpful in designing longer sessions.

6) *The use of creative activities:* The list of basic supplies includes a number of craft materials. It is essential that the leadership team be familiar with the materials. Schedule a day to play and to have some fun experimenting with the several materials. When using various media, remember it is the process not the product that is important; schedule enough time to fit the process. Choose a medium that will help get at the aim or purpose of a particular session or exercise. Look for the issue at stake and choose materials that will illustrate it. If something is to be taken home by the families to be cherished as a special tribute, buy and use good materials. The one rule we have found most helpful in guiding our decisions about any creative activity is "Keep it simple."

CHAPTER 13

Introductions

General Purpose The underlying purpose of the exercises in this section is to create an atmosphere of trust and openness through including and involving everyone in the group. At the beginning of a new program the participants are coming to the sessions full of questions, some of which they may not even know are there: "Who is here?" "Will I know anyone else?" "Can I be myself with my family here?" "Can I be myself with other people here?" "What's going to happen?"

It is important that leaders establish an atmosphere of trust and openness from the very beginning. There is a need to get everyone "on board." A part of this process is to state clearly your expectations and hopes as leaders. Some of this is merely giving information: opening and closing times, meeting place, mealtime routine, etc. One can't assume anything; so it is important to clarify and to answer those hazy questions the participants come with. At the same time it is important to establish an atmosphere which allows any question to arise; there are no silly or dumb questions. In the initial sessions it is important to cover two areas: (1) names—Who is here?; and (2) boundaries—What is the extent of the contract or group agreement? The activities and exercises in this section will help to do these things.

Data and Questions for Leaders During this process the leadership team will be collecting data and re-assessing data from the family visits; this data will determine the exercises for later sessions. Things to watch for include:
  • How are members within a family communicating?
  • How are the several families communicating with one another?
  • How does the chronological age fit with the social development?
  • What kind of "reaching out" ability do you see?
  • What do the family systems look like?
  • Who dominates in the family?
  • Who holds back in the family and in the group?
Look for "red flags," tensions, rules, areas of conflict. All this will determine what is next and how later sessions are to be designed.

Guidelines 1) One whole session should be designed to focus on activities that help participants know one another and to answer their questions.

2) Depending on the openness and trust that is seen and the reaching out that is exhibited, sessions two and three also may include exercises from this Introductions section.

3) Short introductory activities may be built into later sessions. Each time participants leave a group and return, a process of inclusion is necessary. In later sessions this may be a song, a simple game, or the use of stems to sign in (see exercise on page 52).

50

Most participants are coming out of educational models in which they are passive and generally are receiving rather than giving of themselves. There is little experience of inter-generational mixing, and, where there is, often the parents speak *for* the children. There are unspoken questions: "Will my children measure up?" and "Will I measure up?" For most people the experience of the first few sessions will be an orientation to a new educational style. The modeling by the leaders will help to ease the participants into the experience. A key role for the leaders is that of affirming individuals as they participate with others of various ages.

Reminder

Stems

Aim   To provide an opportunity to make transitions.

For   Individuals.

Time   This can be used as an activity while people are arriving. If it is used as an activity within the session, use a limited number of stems, allowing no longer than 20 minutes.

Materials   Large sheets of newsprint or butcher paper, markers or crayons.

Directions   1) Before the group arrives tape sheets to the wall in a position low enough for small children. (If you are using lightweight newsprint, use two thicknesses so that the marking pens won't bleed through to the wall.)

2) On each sheet print one of the following stems:
- We are: (write your name)
- I like to . . .
- I am feeling . . .
- I dream about . . .
- I am wondering about . . .
- Draw a funny face:
- Things people learn from me:
- Ways in which I am like my family:
- Ways in which I am different from my family:

3) As people arrive (or following verbal introductions), ask them to complete each stem. Younger children can be assisted by older ones.

Suggestions for General Reflection   Rarely would you reflect on the stems by themselves. Design the stems so that they begin to focus on the evening's purpose. They can be used as an introduction to a particular activity or as a summary.

It is important to acknowledge some of the information from the stems sometime during the evening.

For Additional Stems See   *100 Ways to Enhance Self-Concept in the Classroom* by Jack Canfield and Harold C. Wells (Englewood, NJ: Prentice-Hall, Inc., 1976).

People Hunt

To discover some interests of other members of the group and to share some of one's own interests. **Aim**

Total group. **For**

15 minutes. **Time**

The "People Hunt" list of questions mimeographed for each person, pencils. **Materials**

Directions

1) Pass out the "People Hunt List" to each participant.

2) Ask each participant to find a person who *best* fits each description and have him or her sign on the corresponding line. Small children may need some help to sign in whatever way they are able, i.e., a picture, a scribble, etc.

3) When completed or at the end of a given time, gather the participants to share their discoveries about the group.

Since this is intended to be a mixer, it is not necessary to spend a lot of time in reflection. To further reinforce the group-building process ask the following questions: **Suggestions for General Reflection**

Did any of you meet someone new?

Did some of you discover likenesses with some of the people here?

Who made a new discovery about someone they thought they knew well?

Would some of you like to explore further some of the information you gathered from people as you met them?

People Hunt List

Your name: _____

Find someone who meets the description on the left and have them sign their name after the description. Get a different signature for each item.

1) Find someone who attends school _____
2) Find someone with blue eyes _____
3) Find someone who was born in another state _____
4) Find someone who likes to ski _____
5) Find someone whose first name begins with a letter from L to S _____ _____
6) Find someone who has been to Disneyland _____
7) Find someone who shares an interest with you _____
8) Find someone who has two or more brothers _____
9) Find someone who takes Spanish or French in school _____
10) Find someone who has a pet _____
11) Find someone who is going to go to college _____
12) Find someone who knows how to play a musical instrument _____
13) Find someone who has read a book just for fun in the last three weeks _____ _____
14) Find someone who has lived in this town all their life _____
15) Find someone who has slept in a tent this year _____
16) Find someone who likes yogurt _____
17) Find someone who has had a broken arm or leg _____
18) Find someone who subscribes to a magazine that is addressed to them _____ _____
19) Find someone who has never been to a scout or Campfire Girl camp _____ _____
20) Find someone who would like to take a trip to the moon _____
21) Find someone who has never been in a play _____
22) Find someone who has a bike or a motorcycle _____
23) Find someone who has done some kind of volunteer work _____
24) Find someone who has a job _____

People Bingo

To provide a quick and light way for the group to mix and to begin sharing on a personal level. **Aim**

Total group. **For**

15 minutes. **Time**

"People Bingo" sheet for each participant, pencils. **Materials**

1) Pass out "People Bingo" sheets to each participant. **Directions**

2) Explain Bingo. You may want to make the object of the game the completion of a series in any one direction or you may want to complete the whole set.

3) Ask participants to find a different person to sign each square. Small children may need some help to sign in whatever way they are able, i.e., a picture, a scribble, etc.

4) When Bingo is called, gather the participants to share their discoveries about the group.

If "People Hunt," pp. 51-52, *has* been used previously, the following questions would be appropriate: **Suggestions for General Reflection**

Did you find seeking out the people to sign your paper an easier task this week? Why?

Whom did you go to first because you knew them a bit already?

What were some new discoveries about people you met last week?

What were the new discoveries about yourself?

Note: If "People Hunt" has *not* been used, then we would suggest using the reflection questions from that exercise.

People Bingo

Find a Person Who . . .

Enjoys rain	Likes pizza	Enjoys mountains	Likes swimming
Likes sleeping bags	Enjoys snow sports	Likes to sew	Enjoys musicals
Likes making things	Enjoys wine and cheese	Likes to tinker	Likes butterflies
Likes to cook	Likes to be alone	Would prefer to have two close friends rather than six casual ones	Likes to be gentle

Hand Stacking

To introduce touch in a non-threatening way and to continue meeting one another on a personal level. **Aim**

Total group. **For**

10-15 minutes. **Time**

None. **Materials**

Directions

1) Gather the group in a tight circle, either standing or seated on the floor.

2) Going around the circle, ask each person to say his or her name and to put his or her right hand in the middle, making a stack of hands.

3) When completed, begin anew using left hands, asking each person to complete the sentence, "I like to . . ."

4) Depending on time, use a variety of statements, such as: favorite food, favorite sport, something I can teach others, age.

Suggestions for General Reflection

If this is used after "People Hunt," pp. 51-52, and/or "People Bingo," pp. 53-54, then the brief reflection could stress any one or a combination of the following areas:

Try closing your eyes and naming all the people who were in your circle.

Whose name and face did you put together for the first time because of this session?

What new discoveries did you make?

Name the person or persons that you want to know better.

Circle Game

Aim   To bring the group together.

For   Whole group.

Time   5 to 10 minutes.

Materials   A list of descriptions prepared by the leader.

Directions

1) Gather the group in a circle.

2) As leader, call out a description and ask those who can respond affirmatively to move to the center. Use your data previously collected to form descriptions so that each person will have at least one opportunity to be in the center. The following are suggestions:

Everyone who goes to school . . .
Everyone who has brown eyes . . .
Anyone who is five or under . . .
Anyone who weighs 100 pounds or more . . .
All who have dogs for pets . . .
Anyone who plays the guitar . . .
All who are hungry . . .

Name those who have responded and ask them to return to a different spot in the circle.

3) Call out a second description, name the participants as they move to the center and return to another spot. Repeat until the list is complete or until you sense the group is ready for a change of pace.

4) Your last description might provide a transition to another activity or exercise.

Interview

To introduce family units to the group. **Aim**

Family groups. **For**

10 minutes for interview, 10 minutes for introduction. **Time**

Set of interview questions. **Materials**

1) Pair families and ask them to interview each other. You may wish to use **Directions**
a set of interview questions, such as:
  • What are the names and ages of the family members?
  • What are the talents, skills, and interests the family members bring to the
    group?
  • What is the family looking forward to in this experience?
  • What are some of the favorite sports, hobbies, and interests of the family?

2) Ask each family to decide how it will make the introduction.

3) Ask each family to introduce the other family to the whole group.

What are some new insights about yourself? **Suggestions**
What did you learn from other members of your family? **for General**
What are some likenesses noticed with your family and the other family? **Reflection**
What are some differences?
What came to mind as you listened to the introductions?
What would you like to do, now that you know more about the family units?

Flower Garden

Aim   To provide an opportunity for each person to reflect on and to share uniqueness.

For   Individuals within the family group.

Time   20 minutes for introduction and construction.

Materials   Colored construction paper, scissors, markers, glue, a long strip of butcher paper.

Directions

1) Prior to the session, tape a long piece of butcher paper to the wall. For each person, draw a flower stem with two leaves. Arrange these in family groups and label each group with the family name.

2) Begin the exercise by asking the participants to think about themselves: How they feel about themselves, what colors those feelings suggest, what shapes those feelings suggest.

3) Let each person choose a color and ask him or her to cut a flower in a shape which suggests his or her feelings. Give each family a different color for centers (these may be pre-cut 2" circles).

4) When the flowers are completed, direct the participants to glue them on the pre-drawn stems. Ask each person to write on one leaf something he or she likes to do and on the other leaf something he or she is good at.

5) When completed make a tour of the garden.

Suggestions for General Reflection
What are some likenesses you see in the whole garden plot?
What are some of the differences in the garden?
What are some of the differences in the plots with the same name?
What does this garden tell you about our whole group?
What are some new learnings, insights, hopes, or frustrations?

Building & Visiting

To continue the group-building process by providing an opportunity for families to share who they are as family units. **Aim**

Family groups. **For**

20-30 minutes for building the house, 30-45 minutes for visiting the homes. **Time**

Large sheet of newsprint for each family, crayons. **Materials**

1) Pass out supplies to each family group. **Directions**

2) Ask each family group to draw their home any way they wish. Include family name and address. Ask each person to indicate his/her favorite spot in the home. Suggest that each family add anything special about their home that they would like to share.

3) When the plans are completed ask each family to take turns visiting other families, sharing the drawings of their home.

4) When the tour is completed gather the group for reflection.

How did you feel as you visited the other homes? **Suggestions**
What are some likenesses your family has with other families? **for General**
How does it feel to "live in the same neighborhood" one evening a week? **Reflection**

Family Construction

Aim   To provide an opportunity for families to share some aspects of their family life.

For   Family groups.

Time   20 minutes for construction, 30-45 minutes for sharing.

Materials   A bag of clean recycled objects (such as plastic vegetable cartons, tin cans, string, tissue rollers, cottage cheese cartons, etc.) for each family.

Directions   1) Ask each family to talk about the following questions:
  • How do we see our family?
  • What are our hopes and dreams for the family?
  • What is it like to be in our family?

Then ask them to decide how they could *construct something* to express their answers.

2) Give each family a bag of supplies and ask them to complete the construction.

3) Ask each family to share its construction.

Suggestions for General Reflection   What did you learn about your family?
What are some questions you have for any of the other families?

Variations   a) Ask each family to draw a tree expressing who they are. Each branch could be drawn in response to a particular question.

b) Give each family some clay to model a description of itself.

c) Give each family pictures and words cut from magazines to make a collage to respond to particular questions.

Variations for Introductions

1) *What family means to me.* Ask each family member to write on a large heart a phrase or statement to complete, "Belonging to our family means . . ."

2) *Family commercial.* Ask each family to prepare a commercial describing the family. Suggest that they think of the advantages, the high points, the excitements that are part of belonging to the family.

3) *Family portrait.* Ask each family to draw a family group portrait including each member and the family pets.

Directions

CHAPTER 14

Communication

General Purpose

The purpose of this section is to provide new tools in the area of communication, together with experiences in using them. These exercises provide opportunities for families to explore present communication patterns and to test options and possibilities for change. Some of the exercises focus on developing skills and processes for clearer communication.

Data and Questions for Leaders

To help you select and order the experiences from this section we suggest focusing and organizing data in the following areas:

Speech Patterns: Are people free to speak for themselves? Note the use of "I" statements as opposed to sentences beginning with "you," "it," "they," or "we," such as, "*I* am angry" rather than "*you* make me angry." "*We* are having so much fun" may not reflect the feelings of the whole group; "*I* am having fun" describes one's own feelings. Are individuals able to own and state their feelings and thoughts?

Hearing and Listening: Do individuals feel free to ask for clarification and further information? Are people listening actively?

Body Language: Do people have eye contact when communicating with one another? Are individuals giving *one* message with their words, facial expressions, and body language? An example would be: "I am glad to be with you," accompanied by a smile and a relaxed body position. A double or *mixed* message would be: "I am glad to be with you," accompanied by a tense body moving away from the other person and an unsmiling, cold expression.

Guidelines

Virginia Satir concluded after many years of experience in working with families that ". . . communication is the greatest single factor affecting a person's health and his relationship to others."[1] Thus, we see the exercises in this section as basic, as prerequisites for the experiences in the following sections. You may find that even after moving on to another area you will need to provide specific opportunities to deepen an understanding or to sharpen a tool needed for open and clear communication.

Reminder

A key function of leadership is to provide a model for the participants. In the area of communication, modeling by the leaders begins as the families gather and continues throughout the session and the whole series. Your open, direct, and affirming communication helps provide an atmosphere of trust and caring, as well as a behavior model from which people can learn.

Suggestion

Read pp. 54-71 in *Changing with Families.*[2]

---

1. Virginia Satir, *Peoplemaking* (Palo Alto, CA: Science & Behavior Books, Inc., 1972), p. 58.
2. R. Bandler, J. Grinder, and V. Satir, *Changing with Families* (Palo Alto, CA: Science & Behavior Books, Inc., 1976).

Fuzzies/Pricklies/Willies/Bugs

Aim

To provide an opportunity to get in touch with feelings about some aspects of family life.

For

Small groups.

Time

60 minutes.

Materials

None.

Directions

1) As an introduction, talk about:
    Fuzzies—good feelings or situations that make us feel good.
    Pricklies—situations that make us feel not so good.
    Willies—situations and things we wonder about.
    Bugs—situations and things that really "bug" us.
Get examples from the group for each.

2) Divide the participants into several small groups, splitting up family members, but maintaining a mix of adults, teens, and younger children in each group.

3) In each small group ask the parents to gather in an inner circle and to share with one another those Fuzzies, Pricklies, Willies, and Bugs they have about their children. Have the younger members in the outer circle listen.

4) At the end of a given time, exchange places and roles in each small group—so that the teens and younger children form an inner circle and share the Fuzzies, Pricklies, Willies, and Bugs they have about their parents while the adults sit silently in an outer circle.

5) Direct the participants to share with the small groups any reactions, responses, or questions raised by the sharing of Fuzzies, Pricklies, Willies, and Bugs.

6) Ask the small groups to share any insights and learnings that have surfaced.

Suggestions for General Reflections

Which of the four situations was easiest to share?
What did you learn about yourself as you shared your Fuzzies, Pricklies, etc.?
What did you learn as you listened to the other groups?

Communication #1

Aim   To explore the effect of physical position on communication.

For   Pairs.

Time   10-15 minutes in each experience.

Materials   One chair per person.

Directions   1) Introduce the exercise by explaining that this is a series of short experiences to explore the effects of physical positions on communication. As leader, you will be directing the experiences, serving as time-keeper, and guiding the reflection.

2) Arrange the group in pairs—adult and child. (You might ask each child to choose an adult or older teen.)

3) *Experience #1*: Ask each child to stand on a chair or bench and his or her adult partner to kneel beside the chair. Ask them to make eye contact but not to change body positions. Instruct them to begin a conversation by sharing their day. After a few minutes, stop the conversations and ask each pair to get into a comfortable position and to reflect on their comfort and feelings during this experience.

Experience #2: Arrange each pair on chairs placed back-to-back a few inches apart. Direct them to begin a conversation. After a few minutes ask them to move their chairs a few feet apart and to continue the conversation. Every few minutes stop the conversation and direct the pair to move their chairs further apart until they lose contact. After contact is lost, ask each pair to move to a comfortable position and to reflect on their comfort and feelings during this experience.

Experience #3: Arrange each pair facing each other, a few inches apart. Ask them to continue a conversation. After a few minutes ask them to move back a little. Continue to stop every few minutes and direct them to move further apart until they lose contact. When contact is lost, ask each pair to move to a comfortable position and to reflect on their comfort and feelings during this experience.

Suggestions for General Reflection   What positions were most comfortable? Why?
What positions were least comfortable? Why?
What did you learn during (name a specific experience)?
Do any of these situations occur in your family?

Communication #2

To increase awareness of the ways in which we communicate verbally and non-verbally. **Aim**

Pairs and trios. **For**

10-15 minutes for each experience. **Time**

None. **Materials**

Directions

1) Introduce the exercise by explaining that this is a series of short experiences to explore verbal and non-verbal communication. As leader, you will be directing the experiences, serving as time-keeper, and guiding the reflection.

2) Arrange the group in pairs and decide who will be A and who will be B.

3) *Experience #1*: One leader gathers all the A's and asks each of them to think of something special to tell their partners. The other leader gathers all the B's and instructs them that they are not to listen to their partners. Bring the partners together and direct A's to begin. Stop. Reflect on feelings.

Experience #2: Arrange the pairs back-to-back and ask them to carry on a conversation. Stop the conversations and direct the partners to face one another and to reflect on feelings in this experience.

Experience #3: Arrange the pairs face-to-face. Ask them to try not communicating for 60 seconds. Stop and reflect on feelings in this experience.

Experience #4: Rearrange the total group into trios and decide who will be A, B, and C. Ask A and B both to talk to C at the same time and ask C to try to respond to them. Stop and reflect on feelings. Change roles. Let each person have a turn at C.

What were some clues to tell you that your partner wasn't listening? How did you feel? **Suggestions for General Reflections**

What makes back-to-back conversation difficult for you?

What was communicated in facial expression and body movement?

How did you feel trying to respond to two people at once?

How did you feel when listening to C's responses?

Design a Game

Aim   To discover how the family works together.

For   Family groups.

Time   30 minutes to design games, 30 minutes to play games.

Materials   A bag of recycled materials for each family, pencils, and paper.

Directions   1) Give supplies to each family.

2) Ask each family to design a game. In planning they are to name the game, to state the purpose or goal of the game, and to develop the necessary instructions.

3) After the games have been designed, direct the families to share the games with one another.

4) If time allows, each family might play all the games designed by other families.

5) Upon completion of the games ask each person in the family unit to reflect on the following questions:
How did we work together in designing a game?
How did we work together in playing a game?
How were the various ideas used?
How were the directions given and received?

Suggestions for General Reflection   What did you discover about working together as a family?
What did you discover as you played together as a family?
What happened as you reflected in your family?

Silent Construction

To discover ways we communicate non-verbally, and to become aware of ways family members influence one another. **Aim**

Family groups. **For**

30 minutes. **Time**

A bag of recycled materials for each family. **Materials**

1) Arrange the participants in family groups. **Directions**

2) Give each family a box of supplies and ask them to construct something together *without talking.*

3) Ask the family members to reflect on the following questions:
What were each of you trying to build?
What did you see in the construction?
How did each of you feel during the construction?
How did you feel when it was completed?
In what ways did you get your ideas across?
In what ways did you fail to communicate your ideas?

How did the silence affect your constructions? **Suggestions**
What did you discover about non-verbal communication in your family? **for General**
How would verbal communication have helped your construction? **Reflection**

Use a simple puzzle and give each member some of the pieces. Each member may add pieces to the puzzle or give pieces to another member, but he or she may not take any pieces from another's pile. **Variation**

Tinker Toy Construction

Aim   To explore communication within the family.

For   Family groups.

Time   45 minutes.

Materials   A basic set of Tinker Toys for each family group.

Directions

1) Arrange the participants in family units and give each group a set of Tinker Toys.

2) Ask each group to take three minutes to discuss what it might build. At the end of three minutes direct the groups to complete their constructions silently in ten minutes.

3) After this has been done, ask each member of the family unit to reflect, using the following questions:

How did we decide what to build? Who made the decision?
How did each member communicate during the construction?
Who led? Who followed?
How did each member participate?
Describe your feelings.
What did you discover about the way your family works together?

Suggestions for General Reflection   What did you learn about your family's decision-making process?
Did anyone feel unenthusiastic about the decision the family made? How did you deal with that?

70

Picture Description

To increase awareness of the need for clarity in oral communication. **Aim**

Pairs. **For**

30 minutes. **Time**

Simple outline pictures, paper, and crayons (pictures should be kept in folders until used). **Materials**

1) Arrange the group in pairs with a surface for drawing. **Directions**

2) Give one of the partners a simple outline picture; give the other partner paper and crayon.

3) Ask one partner to keep the picture to himself or herself and to describe it verbally without naming any article in the picture and without gesturing with his or her hands. The description is to pertain to lines, shapes, sizes, and space. The second person is to attempt to draw the picture following the directions as they are given.

4) When completed, ask the partners to compare the two pictures.

5) Reverse roles and repeat using another picture.

What would have helped you share your picture more accurately? **Suggestions**
Which did you find hardest, giving the directions or trying to follow them? **for General**
Why? **Reflection**
What did you learn about your own ability to communicate that which is very clear to you but totally unknown to the other person?

Non-Verbal Exploration

Aim To heighten awareness of non-verbal communication and its effect on relationships.

For Pairs.

Time 20 minutes.

Materials None.

Directions

1) Introduce the exercise by explaining "non-verbals"—all those gestures we make with our hands and bodies, the way we use our eyes, and the way we use our faces. Give examples or get examples from the group. These movements and expressions may add to or subtract from the meaning of our words; they may or may not fit our verbal expression. We can see the non-verbals of others.

2) Arrange the group in pairs.

3) Ask each pair first to select a topic about which they have some strong feelings (the election, the current athletic season, a favorite food) and then to discuss their selected topic.

4) After five minutes, stop the conversations and ask each person to list the non-verbals used by the partner.

5) Take some time to share the lists.

Suggestions for General Reflection

What did you learn about your use of non-verbals?
What non-verbals do you use most?
Which, if any, of those do you want to change?

Non-Verbal Games

To heighten awareness of feeling responses to non-verbal communication. **Aim**

Total group. **For**

5 minutes for each experience. **Time**

None. **Materials**

Directions

1) Gather the group in a circle and explain that you will be leading this series of non-verbal experiences by giving some simple directions and by guiding the reflection.

Experience #1: With everyone seated on the floor say, "We are going to play ball," and toss out an imaginary ball. Play long enough so that everyone gets a chance to catch and toss. (With some imagination the ball becomes various sizes and types; some may bounce it, some may toss it, some may play keep-away, some may roll it, etc.) Stop and reflect on feelings. The following questions may be helpful to start the reflection: What part of the ball game did you enjoy most? How did you feel about tossing the ball? about catching?

Experience #2: With everyone standing in a circle and holding hands, ask the participants to close their eyes and say, "We are going to form the waves of the ocean." Begin with a gentle surf, move to a stormy sea, change to a gentle incoming tide, etc., (giving some verbal direction with each change). Stop and reflect on feelings. These questions may be helpful: How much of the time did you feel a part of the ocean? Did you or those beside you determine the action of the waves? How did this make you feel?

Experience #3: Form a circle with everyone standing and holding hands. The only instruction given is "You may choose to move the group or be moved by the group." (Note: If there are small children, add a warning to be conscious of all the people, young and old.) After a few minutes, stop and reflect on feelings. These questions may be helpful: What happened to you? How did you feel?

What did you discover about yourself in any of the experiences? **Suggestion for General Reflection**

Pantomime

Aim   To heighten awareness of the reality of non-verbal communication.

For   Total group.

Time   30-45 minutes.

Materials   None.

Directions

1) Select four volunteers and explain the setting to them: a child brings home a picture he has made at school and is eager to show it to his parent. One volunteer will pantomime the child; the others will pantomime three different responses by the parent. The first is very busy with chores and reacts indifferently. In the second situation the parent "tells" the child he can do better. In the third, the parent is accepting of the child's work.

2) Direct the presentations and thank the volunteers when each has finished.

3) After the pantomimes have been presented, ask the group to tell what was communicated to them by the non-verbals, including how it appeared the child felt with each of the parent's reactions.

Suggestions for General Reflection

Which response did you identify with most?

Which of these situations have you experienced in some way?

What could you do to encourage situation #3 to occur more often?

Trigger Words

To become aware of body response to certain words.   **Aim**

Individuals.   **For**

20 minutes for drawing, 20 minutes for simulated family groups, 20 minutes   **Time**
for family groups.

10 large sheets of paper and a pencil for each participant.   **Materials**

1) Introduce the exercise by sharing your own response to the phrase "I love   **Directions**
you" by drawing a stick figure which shows your facial expression, body response, and "gut" feeling. Share the same kind of illustration for a phrase you
don't like to hear.

2) Ask the participants to illustrate in the same way five words, phrases, or
statements they *like* to hear and five words, phrases, or statements they *don't
like* to hear. Put one illustration on each sheet.

3) Group the participants in simulated families and ask them to share their
illustrations.

4) Ask the participants to gather in their own family units and to share their
"Trigger Words."

Conclude by sharing reactions to Trigger Words from *Making Contact* by Vir-   **Suggestions**
ginia Satir (Millbrae, CA: Celestial Arts, 1976). Flash cards for these words   **for General**
are helpful.   **Reflection**

CHAPTER 15

Self-Worth

General Purpose

In this section the focus is on the individual and his or her uniqueness. The purpose is to provide opportunities for participants to discover, to share, and to be affirmed in their differences and their special gifts. These experiences will help families appreciate and value all the members for themselves and for the richness of their uniqueness.

Data and Questions for Leaders

The following questions will be helpful in discovering the needs individuals and families have in order to feel positive about themselves:

Are people able to express their uniqueness, their gifts, and their talents without apology?

Do individuals and family members affirm and celebrate their own beauty and the beauty in others?

Even when experiencing the human conditions of forgetting, thoughtlessness, lack of awareness of others . . . (you continue the list), do individuals express a positive self-image?

Guidelines

Experiences from this section will be more effective if people have developed some basic communication skills: eye-level contact, "I" statements, owning feelings, the ability to give a single message. The other themes to be explored will be more effective if the self-worth of the individual is internalized and not dependent on some thing or someone in the family or group system.

Reminder

As a leader, your own acceptance of all the many parts of yourself will be a continuing exercise and experience of self-worth for the participants. This and your continued acceptance and affirmation of each one in the group are important resources for people in their process of integrating a positive self-image.

Personal/Individual Uniqueness

To provide an opportunity for each person to name and to celebrate personal uniqueness and beauty. **Aim**

Individuals. **For**

25 minutes. **Time**

A strip of heavy paper 3" x 25" for each person, crayons, magic markers. **Materials**

Directions

1) Distribute supplies to the participants.

2) Ask each person to make a hat that expresses himself or herself, writing one word that says something about his or her personality and decorating it with designs and symbols.

3) When the hats are completed, have the participants share them with the group.

4) Conclude the exercise with a parade, marching around the room singing, "When the Saints Come Marching In."

What were your feelings as you made your hat? **Suggestions for General Reflection**
As you looked at the hats of your family members, what did you feel?
What are some new perceptions regarding your family members and other members of the group?
What are some ways you could continue to keep in touch with your growing uniqueness and beauty? What are some ways you could share this growth with your family?

a) Using the tune, "She'll Be Comin' 'round the Mountain," sing a verse for **Variations** each person with the name and special quality: ". . . and *Kevin* will be *enthusiastic* when she comes . . ."

b) In some churches the Feast of All Saints is celebrated. This exercise could be used as a celebration of all the saints in the group.

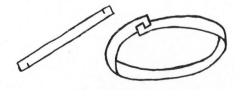

Frog Kissing

Aim   To recognize feelings as facts—neither good nor bad.

For   Family groups.

Time   5-10 minutes for individual work, 20 minutes in family groups.

Materials   A frog cut from colored paper for each person, pencils.

Directions

1) Tell the story of the princess and the frog.

2) Give each person a frog picture with the stem: "I feel 'froggy' when . . ." Ask the participants to write as many endings as they can.

3) Gather in family units and share the responses.

4) Ask the family members to share with each other ways they like to be "kissed."

Suggestions for General Reflection   What are some "froggy" feelings that are the same for two or more persons in your family?

Share some of the ways you like to be "kissed."

Family Uniqueness

To deepen awareness of and to share the uniqueness and special qualities of each family. **Aim**

Family groups. **For**

45 minutes for viewing filmstrip and family groups, 30-40 minutes for sharing. **Time**

The filmstrip entitled *What Kind of Family Has a Pet Joke?*[1] as well as a filmstrip projector and screen, some old clothes for costumes, magic markers, newsprint. **Materials**

1) Show the filmstrip. **Directions**

2) Gather the participants in family units and ask them to discuss family activities in which they all participate: a joke, a rule, a meeting, a game, a celebration, a special activity. Ask them to select one and to plan how this might be shared with the whole group.

3) Ask each family to share its "pet joke" with the others. Allow time for the group to offer its appreciation and to ask any clarifying questions.

How did you feel as you worked together with your family preparing to share with the others? **Suggestions for General Reflection**
What were the likenesses in the activities of the families? What were some of the differences?
What were some insights you gained as you worked with your family or watched what other families shared?

---

1. Filmstrip may be ordered from: Scholastic Book Service, 904 Sylvan Avenue, Englewood Cliffs, NJ 07632. Reference in text used by permission.

I Feel

Aim To provide an opportunity to name one's own feelings.

For Total group.

Time 15-20 minutes.

Materials List of situations for the leader.

Directions 1) Gather the group in a close circle.

2) Read the incomplete sentences from the following list, one at a time, and elicit responses from members of the group. Encourage the participants to repeat the phrase and add their feelings: For example, "When I am tired, I feel cross." Elicit at least two responses to the same incomplete sentence.

For younger children:
When my best friend is naughty, I feel _____
When it is my birthday, I feel _____
When the babysitter comes, I feel _____
When Mommy sits little brother or sister on her lap, I feel _____

For older children:
When the teacher calls on me, I feel _____
When my friend makes a mistake, I feel _____
When Dad or Mom goes on a trip, I feel _____
When I read animal stories, I feel _____

For anyone:
When I'm tired, I feel _____
When I watch a parade, I feel _____
When it's only three days 'til Christmas, I feel _____
When it is raining, I feel _____
When I go to church, I feel _____

For adults:
When I speak before a group, I feel _____
When I'm getting ready to come to family education, I feel _____
When my children fight, I feel _____
When my children draw pictures and give me a token of their love, I feel _____
At a family reunion, I feel _____
When we have company for dinner, I feel _____

3) After some reflection, conclude with one of the following songs: "Free to Be . . . You and Me" or "Get in Touch with the Way You Feel."

What feelings were easiest to name? hardest?

What are some feelings that you haven't been in touch with for a while?

What have been some changes for you in regard to experiencing some of the same feelings through the years?

Family Feelings

Aim To provide an opportunity for family members to share their feelings with one another.

For Family groups.

Time 10 minutes for individual work, 15 minutes for simulated families, 20-30 minutes for family groups.

Materials Paper, pencils, and the "Guide for Asking for Clarification" for each group.

Directions 1) Ask the participants to list as many *family situations* as possible for each of the three statements:

I feel *put down* when . . .

I feel *sad* when . . .

I feel *happy* when . . .

Share some examples for each.

2) Gather in simulated families and ask each person to share his or her list. The others are to listen and may ask clarifying questions but are not to make judgments.

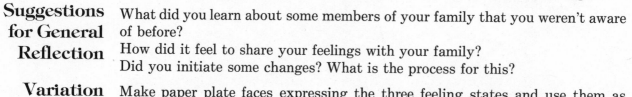

Guide for Asking for Clarification
Do you mean . . . ?
When you say . . ., are you saying . . . ?
I don't know what you mean by . . .

3) Gather in family groups and share in the same way.

4) Ask the family members to discuss: "How I want the family to treat me when I am feeling put down, sad, and happy." Begin to contract for change.

Suggestions for General Reflection What did you learn about some members of your family that you weren't aware of before?

How did it feel to share your feelings with your family?

Did you initiate some changes? What is the process for this?

Variation Make paper plate faces expressing the three feeling states and use them as props or aids in talking about the feelings. Young children can respond more easily with this kind of aid.

Popcorn

To become aware of the differences in people's feelings in a common situation. **Aim**

Total group. **For**

45 minutes. **Time**

Copy of directions for each group. **Materials**

   1) Form the groups and give each group its set of directions. **Directions**

   2) Ask each group to meet and to plan its action.

   3) Direct the groups to begin with "heat" and to move through the actions to the completion of the "popcorn balls."

   4) After reflection, it may be fun to share a big bowl of popcorn.

How did you feel: **Suggestions**
   When you were grouped? **for General**
   When you were named an ingredient? **Reflection**
   When you did your part?
   When people responded to your action/reaction?
   When it was over?
How do you feel now?

   1) Designate one individual to be *maker* of the popcorn. Divide the rest of the **Popcorn Balls** group into ingredients: *heat, oil, popcorn, salt, caramel.*

   2) Explain the action: "Heat warms the oil, heat and oil make the corn pop, popcorn needs salt, etc. . . ."

   3) Each group is given individual help (see group directions below) to decide "how to be heat," "how to be oil," and so on—using body movements and appropriate sounds but no talking.

   4) Action begins when *maker* plugs in *heat.*

Group directions:
   oil
   • You will have to get very hot (with the help of heat) to make the corn pop.
   • Use your whole self to be oil and make all the sounds of oil as your temperature rises.
   • As a group decide how effectively to be oil.
   • Once the action starts it is all without talking.
   heat
   • You must heat the oil and together with the oil heat the corn.
   • You will need to warm the caramel.

- Use your whole self to be the heat and make the sounds of heat.
- As a group decide how effectively to be heat.
- Once the action starts it is all without talking.

popcorn
- When the heat and oil warm you up, you will have to pop.
- You will need to be sprinkled with salt and be stuck together with caramel.
- Use your whole self to be popcorn and make all the sounds of popcorn.
- As a group discuss how effectively to be popcorn.
- Once the action starts it is all without talking.

salt
- After the corn is popped, you will flavor the corn and be bound with it and the caramel to make popcorn balls.
- As a group discuss how effectively to be salt.
- Use your whole self to be salt and make the sounds of salt.
- Once the action starts it is all without talking.

caramel
- You will have to melt, stick to the popcorn and salt, and form two popcorn balls.
- Use your whole self to be caramel and make all the sounds of caramel.
- As a group discuss how effectively to be caramel and to form the other ingredients into two popcorn balls.
- Once the action starts it is all without talking.

My World Collage

To deepen awareness of the uniqueness of personal worlds and to see the need for linking with other worlds.

Aim

Family groups.

For

40-60 minutes.

Time

Picture magazines, glue, scissors, yarn, staplers, and a large cardboard circle for each person (20" to 24" in diameter).

Materials

1) Give each person a cardboard circle and ask him or her to divide it into four sections. Mark the edge of each section with one of the following statements:
   • Who am I?
   • Things I like to do.
   • Things I can share or teach.
   • Things I wonder about.

Directions

2) Ask the participants to find pictures that fit each statement and to attach them in the appropriate section of the circle.

3) After gathering the participants into family groups, ask them to share their "worlds."

4) Ask each person to think about his or her own needs: What do I need from others in my family? What can I learn from other people? What needs do I have that are similar to those of others in my family? Where can these needs be fulfilled?

5) Ask the participants to place their "worlds" close together and ask the family to gather around. Give each person in the family a different colored ball of yarn. Ask them to reflect on their own needs; then ask them to attach one end of the yarn to their own world and the other end to a picture on another family member's world which fulfills a particular need. (Participants may need to cut the yarn in short pieces.)

6) In family units ask them to reflect on the connections demonstrated by the yarn.

What were some feelings and learnings as you linked your world with someone else's?
What are some reactions as you see the separate worlds linked together by needs and wants?
What are some of the things that are the same in all the worlds in your family? What are some of the differences?
As you look at the worlds of the other families, what are some of your reactions?

Suggestions for General Reflection

85

Personal History

Aim To become aware of personal time-lines.

For Individuals.

Time 45 minutes for construction, 30 minutes for sharing.

Materials Long strips of paper for each participant (adding machine tape is easy to use), pencils.

Directions 1) Give a long strip of paper to each person.

2) Ask the participants to think about the significant events, occasions, and accomplishments in their lives (birth, first steps, school, first job, etc.) and any recollections of feelings about the events. Suggest that family members help one another. Direct them to note these events on the long strips of paper beginning with their birth and ending with the present time.

3) After sharing in family groups, tape the strips to the wall. You may want to reflect on similarities and differences in the personal histories.

Note: This exercise is more effective if parents have had the opportunity to share the significance of various events with their children at home and the family comes prepared with some personal and family data.

Suggestions for General Reflection What are some likenesses in all of the time-lines? What are some differences? What are some things we can learn from each other as we live out our time-lines?
What do you hope to see in the time-line of your future?

A Further Suggestion This exercise could provide the initial data for a personal or family scrapbook to which pictures and comments could be added.

Life Size Figures

To heighten awareness of our many parts.

Aim

Pairs.

For

45 minutes for pairs, 20 minutes in family groups, 15 minutes for sharing.

Time

Butcher paper cut the size of each person, markers, crayons, scissors.

Materials

Directions

1) Arrange the participants in pairs, giving each pair two sheets of butcher paper. (This may be a good opportunity for a child to work with an adult from another family.)

2) Ask them to spread the butcher paper on the floor and to have one partner lie on the paper and the other one to trace around him or her with a crayon. Trade positions and tasks.

3) Ask the participants to write the answers to the following questions on their own figures:
  • What are some of the things I can do? (on the right arm)
  • What are some of the ways I am like my family? (on the left arm)
  • What are some of the ways I am not like my family? (on the torso)
  • What are some of the things people can learn from me? (on the head)
  • What are some of the things I don't like to do? (on the right leg)
  • What are some of the things I want you to know about me? (on the left leg)

4) Direct the participants to cut the figure along the outline and with crayons or markers to add facial features and to dress the blank side of the figure. (The youngest children may add only eyes and an indication of clothing; older ones will want to match the clothing they are wearing; adults may be more conscious of features and clothing. The youngest children may need more help to think about uniqueness.)

5) Gather in family groups and ask them to share responses to the questions.

6) You may want to hang the figures from the ceiling or tape them to the wall in family groups.

How did you feel as you were being drawn around?
What was the difference between answering the questions and clothing yourself?
What were some insights and affirmations as you shared with your family?
What did you discover about people tonight?

Suggestions for General Reflection

Feelings Bingo

Aim   To discover the commonality of feelings.

For   Individuals.

Time   10-15 minutes.

Materials   A copy of "Feelings Bingo" for each participant, pencils.

Directions   1) Pass out a "Feelings Bingo" sheet to each participant.

2) Explain Bingo. You may want to make the object of the game the completion of a series in any one direction or you may want to complete the whole set.

3) Ask participants to find a different person to sign each square.

4) When Bingo is called, gather participants to share their discoveries about feelings.

Suggestion for General Reflection   Highlight areas where people often mistakenly think they are alone with their feelings—in order to get at commonality of feelings.

Feelings Bingo

Find someone who feels:

Angry when kids don't pick up their toys	*Contented* when the leaves begin to fall	*Happy* when Friday rolls around	*Nervous* when I have to perform
Sad when a friend is ill	*Glad* when a friend comes to play/visit	*Worried* when the kids don't get home on time	*Loving* when all the family is together
Excited when it is my birthday	*Upset* when family members fight	*Joyful* when fighting family members make up	*Embarrassed* by my mistakes
Silly when I'm tired	*Patriotic* when a band marches by	*Stubborn* when I want something to go my way	*Anxious* in a new situation (school, class, party, etc.)

Family Rituals

Aim To become aware of the riches of the rituals and activities that are special because of history and repetition.

For Family groups.

Time 40 minutes for family groups, 30-40 minutes for sharing.

Materials Craft materials and "dress up" clothes.

Directions 1) Introduce the exercise by talking about traditions and those special events, celebrations, and activities we always do the same way. Share some examples.

2) Gather the participants in family groups and ask each member to think of two special activities, celebrations, or traditions the family does together. Direct each family to compile a list, using each member's contributions.

3) Ask each family to select two items from their list to share with the rest of the group and to decide a way to share them which involves the whole family (pantomime, posters, charades, etc.).

4) Direct the sharing of family presentations, allowing time for the group to express its appreciation and to ask clarifying questions.

Suggestions for General Reflection How did these rituals originate in your family?
What were some additions to the celebration through the years? some deletions? some changes of order? What brought these about?

A Further Suggestion This activity could be continued at home by making a book of Family Rituals and Activities with pictures and comments.

SELF-WORTH

"Pezzettino"

To become aware of shared gifts within a group.   **Aim**

Individual and total group.   **For**

30-40 minutes.   **Time**

Pezzettino[1] by Leo Lionni, large pieces of newsprint, small pieces of colored   **Materials**
paper, glue, markers, or pens.

   1) Read or tell the story of Pezzettino and talk about the many little pieces   **Directions**
that make up each of us. Often we are aware of all those pieces only when we
are told by others.

   2) Ask each person to draw an outline figure and to label it with his or her
name. Tape these to the wall.

   3) Give each person enough pieces of colored paper for every member of the
group. Ask the participants to think about all of the people who are a part of
the group and to write or draw a message for each of them, responding to one
or more of the following:
Something I have learned from you.
Something you have offered for which I am thankful.
A uniqueness you have brought to the group.
A gift you have shared with the group.

   4) Direct them to glue their messages on each of the other figures.

   5) The reflection may be an offering of thanks or a response to individuals
or the whole group.

How did you feel as you wrote messages to your family members? to other   **Suggestions**
people?   **for General**
How did you feel as you read your messages?   **Reflection**
(As individuals share how they feel, ask the group how many others feel this
way. This puts them in touch with the commonality of human feelings.)
What are you going to do with your portrait of your little pieces?

---

1. Leo Lionni, *Pezzettino* (New York: Pantheon Books, 1975). Used by permission.

Treasure Chest

Aim To provide an opportunity for each person to become aware of personal "treasures" and to affirm gifts in others.

For Individuals.

Time 30-45 minutes.

Materials A "treasure chest" for each person and pencils.

Directions

1) Introduce the exercise by suggesting that we are all like chests filled with all kinds of priceless treasures: warmth, fun, hopes, fears, laughter, etc. We know some of our treasures. Others we may be hiding; those hidden treasures may be unknown to us but not to others.

2) Gather the group in a circle and give each person a treasure chest. Ask each person to write his or her name on the chest and to write something special about himself or herself.

3) Direct the participants to pass the chests one person to their right and ask them to write a "treasure" on that chest—some special discovery about that person. Keep passing the chests until the circle has been completed.

4) When the group has finished, gather the participants in family units and ask them to share whatever "treasures" they wish.

Suggestions for General Reflection

What new vision do you have of yourself?
How did you feel when someone was writing on your treasure chest?
How often do you hear good things about yourself?
How often do you tell others good things about themselves?

Group Puzzle

To heighten awareness of the uniqueness of each person's place within the family system. **Aim**

Family groups. **For**

Two hours. **Time**

A piece of plywood at least 4' x 4'. (Cut the plywood into a significant shape; cut that shape into as many pieces as there are people in the group. Mark the bottom side of each piece. Put pieces that fit together in a sack for each family.) Craft materials. **Materials**

1) Give each family a sack with enough puzzle pieces for every person in the family. **Directions**

2) Ask each person to select a piece that is special to him or her. Then ask each participant to decorate the top by writing his or her name and adding any symbols or designs to make it uniquely his or her own.

3) Direct the family units to fit their pieces together.

4) Bring the whole group together and ask the family units to add their pieces to form a single unit.

After the puzzle is together have the group sit around it and note: **Suggestions for General Reflection**
Likenesses and differences.
The beauty this gives.
The necessity of each piece—pick out one piece and talk about how this feels and what happens to the family or the group when one piece is missing.
Reflect on the difficulties in putting the family unit together and the greater difficulties in fitting units to the whole; recall the different options tried.

World Store

Aim To discover the gifts we have to share with others.

For Total group.

Time 30 minutes for small group, 45 minutes for total group.

Materials Large sheet of butcher paper for each group, direction sheet for each participant, markers, crayons, magazines.

Directions 1) Give each participant a direction sheet and ask him or her to list the five items.

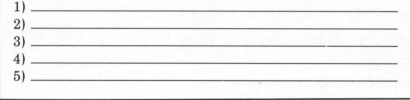

Direction Sheet for World Store

Situation: You are going to open a store that sells things that people want most in the world. Write down the things you think people want and that you could personally offer.

1) _____
2) _____
3) _____
4) _____
5) _____

2) When the lists are completed arrange the group in simulated families and ask the participants to share their lists. Ask the group to select ten items for their store. Direct each group to make a poster indicating the name of their store, their ten items, and some advertising slogan.

3) Share the posters with the total group.

Suggestions for General Reflection
How do you feel about the list of items for your store?
What item in another store would you like to buy?
How do you feel about your gifts being advertised to the world?

Variations a) You could make this a values exercise by shifting the emphasis to "What you think people want."

b) Instead of arranging participants in simulated families, they could meet in family groups and be asked to share "What can the *family* offer because of the personal gifts of the family members?"

Johari Window

To share my perceptions of others and to share myself with others.   **Aim**

Individuals.   **For**

20 minutes for individual work, 20-30 minutes for sharing.   **Time**

Johari Window theory,[1] large sheets of butcher paper, markers, envelopes, small   **Materials**
note sheets, glue, pens, or pencils.

1) Introduce the exercise by explaining the Johari Window concept.   **Directions**

2) Ask each person to draw a figure of himself or herself and to glue an en-
velope pocket on the front.

3) Direct the participants to write as many answers as they can to the fol-
lowing questions, using a separate piece of paper for *each answer*.
• What do I wish others would say about me?
• What thoughts and feelings am I not yet willing to share?

4) Gather in small groups and ask the participants to share how they have
seen each other grow during the time together and how they see each other
now. When someone, sharing his or her perception about a particular person,
mentions something written on a slip of paper, ask that participant to take it
out of the pocket and to attach it to the figure.

How did you feel responding to the questions? sharing your perceptions? when   **Suggestions**
your window was opened?   **for General**
What are some ways you could open that window for yourself?   **Reflection**

---

1. Reproduced by special permission from *Human Relations Training News*, "The Johari Window" by Joseph Luft, Volume 5, Number 1, pp. 6-7, 1961. Copyrighted by NTL Institute, 1961.

The Johari Window

A concept developed by Joseph Luft and Harry Ingham

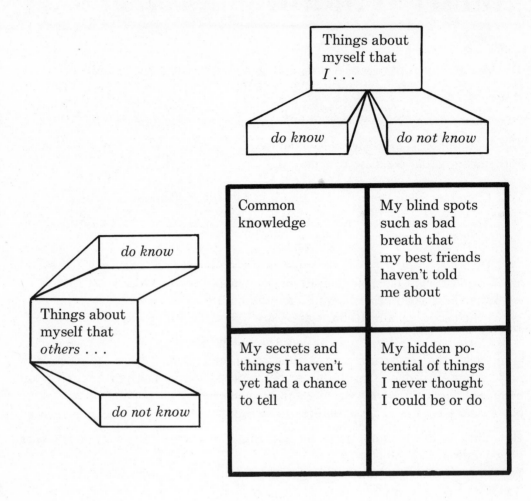

There are some things we know about ourselves and some that we don't know. There are some things that others know about us and some things they don't know. For you and any other person this can be represented by a diagram known as the Johari Window.

As you develop a sharing or helping relationship with another person—a relationship where each of you helps the other to grow—the blind spot and secret areas become smaller as more information about each other becomes common knowledge. It is not meant to be implied that a person should be completely or indiscriminately open. There are things about each of us that aren't relevant to the sharing or helping relationships we have with others. As those things that are relevant are shared, and as they are found to be helpful, a trust develops that allows us to explore and discover new abilities in our area of hidden potential. This is where growth and discovery occur.

CHAPTER 16

Family System

All the exercises in this section focus on the family as a system. These activities explore *system*, the *family system* in general, ways of examining a *particular* family system, and the unlimited options for becoming an *open system*. The specific areas within family system that are experienced and reflected upon include: roles and functions within the family, feelings, outside influences, and pressures. These experiences are designed to give the families skills and tools to enable them to develop the processes for opening and humanizing the family system.

General Purpose

As you begin thinking of using exercises from this section, think about what you have observed in the various family systems.
- Are all members of families accepted as vital parts of a whole, even the person in the womb?
- Are roles and functions, rules and communication designed for balance and movement within the system?
- How are age and sex viewed within the systems?
- What needs are there to enable systems to become more linear and less hierarchical in structure?
- What space is allowed for change and movement by individuals within the system?

Data and Questions for Leaders

The firmer the foundation is for congruent communication and positive feelings of self-worth, the deeper families will be able to go in the exploration of their structures. You may find it helpful to provide some short communication and personal affirmation exercises as a prelude to family system experiences.

Guidelines

It is possible for persons and systems to change and to grow. Your task is one of facilitating this process. It is crucial for you and the families that you not judge a system "open" or "closed," and that you continue to affirm all members of the system as they explore and try out new behaviors. The experiences in this section begin a process of becoming a more humanizing family system that, it is hoped, will continue through generations.

Reminder

Read chapter 8 in *Peoplemaking*.[1]

Suggestion

1. Virginia Satir, *Peoplemaking* (Palo Alto, CA: Science & Behavior Books, Inc., 1972).

Hats We Wear

Aim To become aware of the many roles and functions within the family system.

For Family groups.

Time 20 minutes to make hats, 10-15 minutes in simulated families, 45 minutes in family groups.

Materials Paper strips 2" x 25" (allow 5 to 10 per person), markers, crayons.

Directions

1) Introduce the exercise by talking about the many "hats" we wear in the course of a day. Share some examples.

2) Give several strips to each person and ask the participants to make a hat for each role they fulfill in their family by labeling the strip of paper with the role: bread-baker, garbage-man, babysitter, dishwasher, lawn-raker, etc. (note: mother, father, brother, and sister are not roles).

3) When the participants have finished, have them gather in simulated families and ask each person to share by putting on:
- all his or her hats.
- the hat liked best (and tell how he or she feels when wearing it).
- the hat liked least (and tell how he or she feels when wearing it).
- the hat worn most often (and tell how he or she feels when wearing it).

4) Gather in family units and share as above.

5) After sharing, direct the family to discuss the following questions: Are all these roles needed in our family? Can any of them be fulfilled by different people? What changes in roles and functions would be helpful in our family?

6) Begin contracting for change.

Suggestions for General Reflection
Share learnings about roles and functions.
Share processes used for changes being made.

Picture Gallery

To discover where I am in the family setting and where I'd like to be. **Aim**

Family groups. **For**

5-10 minutes to tour, 15 minutes in simulated families, 20 minutes in family groups. **Time**

Leaders should look for photos of family groups in various picture magazines. Look for photos of families doing things together: playing, eating, working, etc. Try to get a great variety of activities, particularly ones with varying physical positions. Mount these photos and place them around the room. **Materials**

1) As the group tours the photo gallery, ask each person to select one picture that best describes "Where do you see yourself now?" and to select a second picture that best describes "Where would you like to be?" **Directions**

2) Gather in simulated families and ask participants to share their choices and reasons for making the choices.

3) Gather in family groups and ask each person to share his or her choices and reasons for making the choices. During this sharing, the participant should state also what is needed to get to where he or she would like to be—and then ask for what is needed. Family members asked are to respond in the way most appropriate for them.

4) Together the family makes an agreement for change for a limited period of time and agrees to evaluate the situation at the end of that time. This contracting process is done for each family member who wishes to initiate change.

What are some discoveries about yourself? **Suggestions**
What are some discoveries about other family members? **for General**
What are some things you discussed or contracted in your family? **Reflection**

Outside Influences

Aim To provide an opportunity to examine the many influences coming into the family system.

For Family groups.

Time 30 minutes for individual work, 45-60 minutes for family groups.

Materials Large paper circles for each person (at least 22" in diameter), crayons, magazines, glue, scissors, yarn, etc. A larger paper circle for each family unit.

Directions

1) Ask each person to find pictures and to make a collage expressing the influences on his or her life other than those given by the family. Each person should look for pictures that express: places he/she goes, TV he/she watches, people he/she is with, things he/she does, games he/she plays, movies he/she sees, ways in which he/she spends time.

2) Gather the participants in family groups and ask them to share the individual collages.

3) Direct each family group to use the large circle and to write on it the influences they share in common. What are the values underlying these influences?

4) Direct the family units to tie their individual collages together around the "family" circle.

5) Ask each family to discuss their value system using the following questions: How does each member contribute to the family value system? How do personal values conflict with family values?

Share any insights about influences that work against the family value system. How is the family affected by outside influences?

Suggestions for General Reflection

Are there some influences coming into your family that you were unaware of until this evening?

What are some new understandings and appreciations regarding the various value systems within your family?

Any reactions to other family collages?

Rules #1

To provide an opportunity to review rules in the family. **Aim**

Family groups. **For**

10 minutes for individual work, 20-30 minutes for family groups. **Time**

Paper and pencils for each participant, 1 copy of the questions (given below) **Materials**
for each person, 1 Rule Check List for each small child.

1) Ask each person working individually to write down all the rules that are **Directions**
operative in his or her family. It is helpful if young children use the Rule Check
List and are assisted by the leaders.

Rule Check List

Name: _____

Bedtime rules:

Eating rules:

Play rules:

Clean-up rules:

Playmate rules:

Other rules:

---

2) Gather the participants in family units and ask them to take turns reading
their rules. Only clarifying questions (see page 82) may be asked during the
sharing.

3) Distribute sheets with the following questions which are adapted from

Peoplemaking.[1] Ask the families to discuss their rules using these questions as a guide.

- How are the rules made in our family? Does just one of us make them? Is it the person who is the oldest, the nicest, the most handicapped, the most powerful?
- Does our family get them from books? from the neighbors? from the families where the parents grew up? Where do they come from?
- What has our family worked out for making changes in the rules? Who is allowed to ask for changes?
- The legal system of our country provides for appeals. What is the appeal system in our family?

Suggestions for General Reflection

What are some discoveries about rules in your family?
What are some changes you hope for?
How will you make those changes?

---

1. Virginia Satir, *Peoplemaking* (Palo Alto, CA: Science & Behavior Books, Inc., 1972), pp. 97-98. Used by permission.

Rules #2

To be aware that unwritten rules, though invisible, are a powerful force in the family. **Aim**

Family groups. **For**

10-20 minutes for individual work, 30 minutes for family groups. **Time**

A copy of Rule Sheet #2 for each participant, pencils (younger children will need special help, including perhaps the suggestion to illustrate their responses). **Materials**

1) Distribute Rule Sheet #2 and ask each person to complete it. **Directions**

Rule Sheet #2

What can you say in your family about what you feel, think, see, hear, smell, touch, and taste? Can you comment only on what should be rather than what *is*? Can you express your fear, loneliness, helplessness, anger, need for crying, tenderness, aggression, and so on?

What are the rules in your family regarding the expression of *anger*?

What are the rules in your family for expressing *disagreement* or *disapproval* of someone or something?

What are the rules for *asking for clarification* when another family member doesn't make himself/herself understood? (Is the rule, "If *you* don't understand *me*, it is always because of *you*"?)

What are the rules in your family for thinking about, talking about, questioning *sex*?

What are the rules in your family for expressing *affection*?

---

2) Gather the participants in family units and ask them to share their responses. While each person is sharing, only clarifying questions (see page 82) may be asked.

3) When the responses have been read, ask each family to discuss its rules in light of the following questions:[1] What do we think about our rules? In what

---

1. Questions have been adapted from Virginia Satir's work *Peoplemaking* (Palo Alto, CA: Science & Behavior Books, Inc., 1972), pp. 98-99. Used by permission.

way are they most overt, human, and up-to-date? In what way are they most covert, inhuman, and out-of-date? How can we plan to work on our rules as a family?

Suggestions for General Reflection

What rules show the greatest variety of responses in your family?

What was helpful in the exercises completed in Rules #1 for tonight's exercise?

Mobiles

To heighten awareness of the presence of a system within the family. **Aim**

Family groups. **For**

60 minutes for construction, 30 minutes for sharing. **Time**

Different sizes and shapes of heavy tagboard and/or light plywood—one for each participant—roll of fishline, pieces of doweling in various lengths, and markers. **Materials**

1) Ask each participant to choose one piece of tagboard or plywood and to add his or her name and decorate it. **Directions**

2) Direct each family to hang the main piece of doweling from the ceiling at a height that is convenient for the family to reach.

3) Direct the parents to attach and balance their pieces. As they attach them, ask the parents to share with the family some of the adjustments they had to make when they married.

4) Add another doweling and direct each child, beginning with the oldest, to attach his/her piece and to balance the mobile. As each child adds his/her piece, ask the family to talk about the adjustments the family made at the time of that child's birth. Continue to add pieces and share adjustments until everyone has finished. You may want to add anyone else living in the home, as well as pets.

5) The following suggestions may help to continue the discussion:
• Find another way to achieve the same balance.
• Mom is sick, and the system is unbalanced (wind her piece up a bit). Re-balance your family system, sharing ways the family could help during the illness.

What were some of the frustrations you felt as you were balancing your mobile? **Suggestions**
What insights came out of the frustrations? **for General**
What are some discoveries about your family that came from sharing the symbols or in the balancing? **Reflection**
Do you have any other reactions to the mobiles?

Conflict Bingo

Aim To create an atmosphere of openness in sharing conflict situations.

For Total group.

Time 10 minutes.

Materials Conflict Bingo" sheet and pencil for each participant.

Directions 1) Pass out a "Conflict Bingo" sheet to each participant.

2) Explain Bingo. You may want to make the object of the game the completion of a series in any one direction or you may want to complete the whole set.

3) Ask the participants to find a different person to sign each square.

4) When Bingo is called, gather the participants to share their discoveries about conflict.

Suggestion for General Reflection Highlight areas where people often mistakenly think they are alone in a conflict situation—in order to get at commonality.

106

Conflict Bingo

Find a person who fights about:

Doing dishes	TV programs	Cleaning up a shared room	The last piece of cake
Eating vegetables for dinner	What game to play	Going out in the evening versus staying home	How money is spent
Babysitting	Privacy	Others helping themselves to his/her things	Doing homework
Disciplining the kids	Using the bathroom (and all the hot water)	Going to bed	Coming in from play

Role Reversal

Aim To share alternatives for common conflict situations.

For Total group.

Time 60 minutes.

Materials List of situations.

Directions 1) Gather the total group in a circle, sitting on the floor with an open space in the center. Explain the process: There will be a series of situations that are common family problems; as simulated families, they are to work toward solutions for the problems. In this setting the roles will be reversed with children playing parents and adults playing children. You may want to announce the simulated family groups and give them a few minutes to be together.

2) Ask the first group to come to the center and give them their situation; remind them that the roles are reversed. While they are playing the situation, one of the leaders could list on newsprint the solutions suggested.
Some possible situations:

- Teenagers want to congregate at Bob's Drive-In after the basketball game; parents are doubtful about it.
- A 13-year-old wants to date; a 17-year-old sister already has dating privileges; take a stand either with or against sibling.
- There is a constant conflict over doing the supper dishes.
- It is Saturday afternoon with two children playing a game and having a dispute over the rules.
- It is a school night after dark; the little children want to go play hide-and-seek in the street.
- Each child has a favorite TV show at the same time on different channels, and there is only one TV set.
- It is supper time, and the family is gathered at the table; one child refuses to eat the vegetables.
- Two children share a bedroom, and it needs its Saturday cleaning.
- It is time to mow the lawn. No one can remember which youngster did it last, and they all have something else they want to do.

3) After a few minutes, stop the action and thank the players. Involve the whole group in discussing the suggested solutions. Then move to the next situation played by another simulated family.

Suggestions for General Reflection In reflecting on the situations, ask about feelings in the conflict situations and how they felt about playing the other role.
How did you feel about the various suggestions that were offered as solutions?
How did you feel about the final solution?

Situation Changing

To open discussion on conflict areas within the family and to provide an opportunity to change a conflict situation. **Aim**

Family groups. **For**

5-10 minutes for individual work, 10-15 minutes in simulated families, 30-45 minutes in family groups, 20 minutes for sharing. **Time**

Paper and pencil for each person. **Materials**

1) Ask each participant to list the things or situations that he or she feels **Directions** cause conflicts or problems in the family. Ask each person to suggest what he or she would like to have happen in each of the situations listed.

2) Arrange the participants in simulated families and ask them to share their lists and suggestions. As each person shares, the others may make comments or ask clarifying questions (see page 82), but they are not to make judgments.

3) Move the participants into family groups and ask each person to share his/her list. Again, clarifying questions are acceptable but judgments are not.

4) Direct each family group to choose one situation to share with the total group. In sharing they are to tell how the situation is perceived by each family member; how, as a family, they are going to change it; and when they are going to evaluate the change. The sharing can be done by a poster, pantomime, dramatization, etc.

What did you discover about conflict situations in your family? **Suggestions**
What did you discover about conflict situations as you shared in simulated **for General**
families? **Reflection**
Do you have any reactions to projected changes in other families?

CHAPTER 17

Celebration & Closure

General Purpose

Dag Hammarskjold wrote, "For all that has been, Thanks; for all that will be, Yes." Each session and all events come to an end. The purpose of the exercises in this section is to affirm and celebrate a time of growth and to acknowledge an ending or closure to this part of the growth process.

Data and Questions for Leaders

As the group reaches the end of the agreed number of sessions, the leadership team needs to be sensitive to the process of closure. The entire final session, and perhaps the last two, will revolve around this issue. In planning activities and exercises you will want to note the spirit and style of the group and plan accordingly. What is the trust level of the group? Don't go beyond it. In a church related group the closing activities might be biblically or theologically oriented. Help to make the links with the Judeo-Christian backgrounds of the community, with growth and creativity. In groups that are not a part of the church community, the leaders might find stories or myths that speak to these same issues.

Although the activities in this section speak to the ending of a series, each session needs some closure. Plan each evening with a brief activity that says, "This is the end." It may be a summary; it may be pulling together and noting highlights, learnings, or questions. In some groups a prayer circle is appropriate. For others, a particular song may express the spirit of the group and be appropriate to the end of the sessions.

Little celebrations along the way are helpful. Remember birthdays, anniversaries, or special events in the lives of the members. Often the meal shared together is the appropriate setting for these celebrations.

Guidelines

Be sensitive to the inter-generational make-up of the group in language, style, and tasks. It is easy to move into planning something that is too "adult" in concepts. Allow enough time for personal expression of thanks—to each other and to the leadership team—for the activities and for opportunities to explore and grow. Some of the thanksgiving may have to be modeled by the leaders, yet it is important to allow the participants to offer their thanks in a manner appropriate to who they are. This "goodbye" should allow for the next "hello." Provide people with an address and phone list. Help them to plan a post-session gathering, if that is appropriate, or assist them in moving into a network of others who have participated in multi-family groups. Allow some time to explore the next steps.

It is sometimes appropriate to end with a gift to each member—a token that speaks to the on-going process of growth and renewal: an issue of *Mushroom Family*, a poster, or a calligraphed saying, etc. Often these gifts can be a means of helping people to see how this experience can be taken back into the world of daily living. This is especially important for participants in weekend or week-

110

long experiences. For some people this is a mountain-top experience, and they will need to see the way down the mountain and into the valley.

Each session needs some closure. The ending of a series or a weekend needs special attention and care.

Reminder

Celebration means many things to different people. Help the group to share and acknowledge the giving-of-thanks for the life shared.

Some families need to find ways of having fun together and ways of sharing. They may see different models by the several family units.

It is especially important for a leadership team to take time for celebration and closure for themselves. Much time and energy has been invested, and it is important to acknowledge personal growth. The team may want to review personal goals and acknowledge how these were achieved or changed along the way. There is some thanksgiving that you will want to offer with the group and some that will be a part of team life alone.

Pot Filling

Aim To affirm each person in the group.

For Total group.

Time 60-90 minutes.

Materials A large grocery bag for each person, crayons, small pieces of paper (each person needs a packet equal to the number of the total group), pencils.

Directions

1) Tell the story of the old iron pot (see *Peoplemaking*, p. 20).[1]

2) Give each person a paper bag and ask him or her to decorate it with his or her name and appropriate designs or symbols.

3) Gather the participants in a circle and explain that we are going to fill each other's "pots" by writing messages of appreciation to each person in the group. This is a special time to share the "Good News" we have heard through one another. (Note: Younger children may draw pictures.)

4) One at a time each participant sits in the center of the circle with his or her "pot." The others on the outside write a note and drop it in the pot. This is also the opportunity to say the special "thank-you's" and to give a hug.

---

1. Virginia Satir, *Peoplemaking* (Palo Alto, CA: Science & Behavior Books, Inc., 1972), p. 20. Used by permission.

Light to the World

To emphasize that uniqueness is a gift to be developed. **Aim**

Total group. **For**

30 minutes. **Time**

A small low table, white cloth, large candle, small tapers or vigil candles for **Materials**
each person, flashlight, Bible.

1) Gather the whole group around the table and then sit on the floor. **Directions**

2) After a few minutes of silence, turn off the lights and begin the First Reading (John 1:1-5,9).

3) Light the large candle in the center of the table and continue with the Second Reading (I Cor. 12:4-11,27).

4) Call each person by name and ask him/her to come to the center; present each person with a lighted candle in appreciation of his/her uniqueness and specialness: "Thank you, Karen, for giving the gift of your awareness and sensitivity to each person here. You bring more love-light into the world."

5) After each person has received a symbol of his/her light, continue with the Third Reading (Matthew 5:13-16).

6) Conclude the celebration with a song the group has found to be its special song.

CHAPTER 18

Transitions

General Purpose

The short activities in this section are intended to be used as warm-up exercises to begin an evening session or as a means of changing the pace or mood in the group.

Data and Questions for Leaders

Some of these activities can be planned as a means of separating two major exercises of an evening session. There are other times when the energy level in a group drops, and an activity is needed to pick up the excitement. Sometimes a light touch is needed, and an action song is appropriate. The spirit of the group is the data; be sensitive to it and be ready to respond accordingly.

Often groups develop favorites, and a session just can't end until the favorite song is sung or until the special game is played. The children may have suggestions; be ready to let them offer their choices.

Guidelines

Have a ready supply of these short games and activities. With the help of a guitarist, there are a number of songs that are easily used to change the pace.

A Variety Pack

To warm up the group or to change the pace or mood.

Total group.

5-10 minutes each.

Words to songs or verses are needed in some of the activities.

1) *Balloon Race*: Arrange the participants in groups of six to eight people and ask them to form circles. Give each circle a balloon and, at the starting signal, ask them to pass the balloon around the circle three times without using hands. Have fun popping the balloons at the end.

2) *Gossip*: Arrange the group in a circle. Ask one person to begin by whispering a silly sentence, such as "Mickey Mouse wears a striped sweatshirt while skating down a steep curving street," to his or her neighbor. That person whispers the sentence to the third person and so on around the circle. Ask the last person to tell the whole group what he or she heard.

3) *Back-Rubs*: Arrange the group in a circle with one person behind the other. Ask the participants to gently massage the back, neck, and shoulders of the person in front of them. After a few minutes ask everyone to turn around and repeat the gentle massage with a new partner.

4) *Motor Races*: Divide the participants into three groups and arrange each group in a circle sitting on the floor. Group 1 is to be a motorboat and will make a "putt-putt" sound; group 2 is to be a motorcycle and will make a "brr-brr" sound; group 3 will be a race car and will make a "zoom-zoom" sound. Designate one person in each group to begin. That person says the group's motor sound to the person next to him/her who passes the sound to the third person and so on around the circle. The sound passes around the circle three times.

5) *Rabbit Game*: Arrange the participants in a tight group sitting on the floor. Share the verse:

> Rabbit in a bean patch
> Possum in a pot
> Try to stop the fiddler
> While the fiddler's hot.

Ask the participants to alternate slapping knees and clapping hands, keeping the rhythm of the verse. Repeat the verse several times, increasing the speed each time. After a few times through, ask the participants to clap hands and slap knees with a partner on their right; repeat with a partner on their left.

6) *Heads, Shoulders, Knees, and Toes*: Using the tune, "There's a Tavern in the Town," sing the words "Heads, Shoulders, Knees, and Toes." As the parti-

cipants sing each word, direct them to touch the corresponding part of the body. Repeat the verse several times, singing faster each time.

7) *My Bonnie*: Ask the group to sit on the floor and to sing "My Bonnie Lies Over the Ocean." Direct the group to jump up with each word that contains a B.

8) *Harry*: Teach the nonsense verse and after a few times through ask the participants to add the actions (words to the verse are in italics).
Oh (make an O with your fingers), *I* (point to eye), *say* (point to mouth). *Have you heard* (point to ear), *about Harry* (point to hair), *who just* (point to chest), *got back* (point to back), *from the front* (point to stomach), *where he was needed* (knees), *at the foot* (toe), *of the army* (arm)? *Everybody's* (hands up), *heard* (ear), *about Harry* (hair).

9) *Face-To-Face*: Arrange the group in pairs and share the following three directions and actions. When "Face-to-Face" is called, the partners are to face one another; when "Back-to-Back" is called, they are to stand with their backs together; and when "Change" is called, each member is to find a new partner and assume the previous position. The leader should vary the commands and the speed.

10) *A What?*: Arrange the group in a circle with one person designated as leader. The leader hands the person on his/her right an object and says, "This is a dog," and that person replies, "A what?" The leader answers, "A dog," and with the answer the person passes it on saying, "This is a dog." The third person asks, "A what?" and the question is passed back to the leader, and the answer is passed down the line again. The object is passed around the circle to the right with each person receiving it asking the question; the question is passed back to the leader, and the answer is passed down the line. At the same time the leader starts passing a second object to the left with the statement, "This is a cat." It is passed, questioned, and answered in the same manner. The fun begins when the two objects cross.

Suggestions for General Reflection

Usually no reflection is necessary, as the activities are meant to be transitions or warm-ups. A leader might ask, "Are you ready to move on?" or check to see how many were involved.

Further Suggestions

It is helpful to have a number of short exercises ready to use as a change of pace. These activities should be light and should involve everyone; it is especially important to involve the youngest children. Recall childhood party games and activities in Brownie and Cub Scout manuals.

IV Appendices

Care & Nurture of Leaders

Inter-generational group leaders have a need of support. This support, which may come from two directions, is vital to the leadership of the family education group.

There is need for peer support. If several inter-generational groups are meeting, the leaders may want time together to share ideas and plans, to "talk shop." In-service training can be scheduled; the peer support that occurs here may be as important as the training.

As the design of the evening sessions emerges from the group, the in-service training might emerge from the teams. What are the needs? Where are some skills lacking? There might be a need to sharpen planning skills, to sharpen observation skills, to preview films or music, to take a look at some games, or to share some theory regarding family systems. If you are in charge of coordinating the program, you might design the training. If you are a part of a team and see some needs, ask someone who has the appropriate skills to come to help with the training. Look for directors of religious education, counselors in family groups, educators in colleges and universities. Arrange to contract for their time and talent.

A great number of flyers and brochures cross all of our desks. Look at these for opportunities that offer training where, in addition to learning theory, one can learn skills by practice and reflection. Key phrases to look for are laboratory training, experiential education, training in inter-generational models.

Church systems—local, regional, and ecumenical—offer mini-courses, workshops, conferences, and training labs. Look for experiences that offer exposure to family education, cluster groups, inter-generational education. Watch for catalogues and announcements from community colleges, evening courses, extension services. Such titles as conflict management, family systems, assertiveness training, marriage and family enrichment, and group process might offer additional skills for team members. Community organizations such as local mental health associations, Lutheran Family Service, YMCA and YWCA, and other helping agencies often have continuing education opportunities.

In addition to basic training for group work, some events will offer designs that might be adapted for inter-generational groups. When working with families, it is helpful to keep that "bag of designs" growing.

The other level of support comes from the sponsoring agency. If inter-generational group leaders meet with the religious education board (or whoever is the sponsor), there is less danger that the family group will be merely an experimental, pilot, or extra-curricular group.

Look for ways to build an ecumenical exchange of leaders. Explore the pooling of resources and personnel. The advantage or "pay-off" provides peer support as well as aid in building the human community.

A Word about Words

There is no one word or phrase to describe the concept of family education. In our work we have reviewed a series of words and have found that one phrase will capture the imagination of one group, whereas the same phrase will produce nothing within another group. In our writing we have tried to use various words hoping that you will find one that will tag your attention for your time and place. Among the many words and phrases in use are: family education, family and community building, family cluster, inter-generational group, multi-family groups, family enrichment, family development, cluster, intergroup, extended family—and the list goes on.

Whatever the word or phrase, we hope the model will identify or characterize a coming together of persons who want to learn by sharing common experiences.

Other Models

Many people are excited about the possibilities of education within inter-generational groups. Once a person has experienced the excitement and the learning that is possible within such a group, he or she often wants no other kind of educational experience.

We have listened to many people, looked at and experienced other models, read about many more, and are curious about new models which are developing. Most of the models have several themes in common:

1) Several ages or generations are included in the group.
2) Activities are designed for a short term duration.
3) Some kind of contract is made—in which each member agrees to participate for the duration of the sessions.
4) Several families, living units, and single persons are a part of the total group.

The several models fall into one of the following categories:

Variations on the Contract Group

There are models with longer and shorter sessions. The number of sessions varies between four and twelve. In some areas we have found leaders who design programs for one of the seasons of the church year, such as the four weeks of Advent or the six weeks of Lent. In other places we have found models in which the group agrees to meet one Sunday each month during the school year.

There are also variations for leadership. Some groups share the leadership, rotating the responsibility from family to family each week. There are groups in which the decision on content comes from the group itself, with each family or living unit choosing a subject area and planning the activities for a particular session. In other groups a steering committee plans the overall scheme with each session being led by different persons.

Family Camps or Family Weekends

Taking multi-family or inter-generational groups to a conference center or camp setting for two or three days, or even a week, can provide more time for education than is possible during a whole year under ordinary circumstances. The setting away from home and from the cares and concerns of daily living allows a large block of time for teaching and learning. Themes may be developed from a book or film such as *The Little Prince, Nog's Vision, Hope for the Flowers, Arrow to the Sun*, or any of C. S. Lewis' Narnia stories. Generally the families may be expected to have read the book before coming to the experience. Activities, songs, and games help the participants to experience the story. The use of fantasy allows for an easy transition to the teaching and experiencing of theology. Relationships within the family and within the community are strengthened by this kind of experience.

An example of such an experience can be seen in the film, *Journeys: Hopeful Signs in Parish Education*, produced by the Office of Religious Education of the Episcopal Church. To obtain the film, write: David W. Perry, 815 Second Avenue, New York, NY 10017.

Some parishes and churches are doing all of the sacramental preparation in multi-family settings. Once or twice each year several sessions will be scheduled for baptismal preparation; at another time there will be several sessions for preparation for first communion; and at other times there will be sessions preparing for confirmation or reconciliation. Children, parents, godparents, and sponsors are encouraged to attend. In some models the various age groups are separated for a part of each session, with both the adults and children dealing with the same theme. Often there will be a big celebration for the whole parish to conclude the experience.

Sacramental Preparation

In this model one whole day or an afternoon is set aside to make special preparations or to develop special celebrations for one of the seasons of the church year. The day, or even part of one day, allows ample time and opportunity for families to prepare for a season by sharing customs, by learning new skills, or by gaining new insights into old traditions. It is possible to develop learning centers offering several kinds of experiences, ranging from simple crafts to those that are content centered. A family can gather a range of experiences to enrich their celebrations of the season at home. Here are some examples:

Family Days

a) An Advent Festival might include the making of Advent calendars, Advent wreaths, simple creches, wrapping papers, and decorations. Folk songs and folk dancing might be taught.

b) An Easter Celebration might include decorating eggs and the baking of a special Easter bread. A number of Easter symbols lend themselves to banner-making. The day might conclude with a great procession.

c) Activities and materials at a Pentecost Party could include making a birthday cake, wind chimes, releasing balloons filled with messages, as well as decorations and symbols to indicate the coming of the Holy Spirit.

A special day might be centered around the creative arts with experiences in painting, modeling clay, dance, simple crafts, and folk songs. A special day in the summer lends itself to family sports, with each participating family sharing a game. There are many possibilities with music as the special theme for a family day. Some communities have their own special holidays that could provide the theme for inter-generational activities.

In some parts of the country, multi-family groups put education in a secondary place. These groups form with a primary purpose that is either based on pastoral concerns or centered on prayer. The pastoral groups often have a "shepherd couple" who helps people in the group to minister to one another or to the community. Other shepherd groups meet for informal worship and liturgy—sharing a life of prayer.

Shepherd Groups

Bibliography

General Books

Bandler, R.; Grinder, J.; and Satir, V. *Changing with Families*. Palo Alto, CA: Science & Behavior Books, Inc., 1976.

Burns, Marilyn. *I Am Not a Short Adult*. Boston, Toronto: Little, Brown and Company, 1977.

Dodson, Laura Sue. *Family Counseling: A Systems Approach*. Muncie, IN: Accelerated Development, Inc., 1977.

Freire, Paulo. *Pedagogy of the Oppressed*. New York: Seabury Press, 1973.

Satir, Virginia. *Making Contact*. Millbrae, CA: Celestial Arts, 1976.

Satir, Virginia. *Self-Esteem*. Millbrae, CA: Celestial Arts, 1975.

Satir, Virginia. *Peoplemaking*. Palo Alto, CA: Science & Behavior Books, Inc., 1972.

Activity Books

Canfield, J., and Wells, H. C. *100 Ways to Enhance Self-Concept in the Classroom*. Englewood Cliffs, NJ: Prentice Hall, Inc., 1976.

Cole, A.; Haas, C.; Bushnell, F.; and Weinberger, B. *I Saw a Purple Cow: And 100 Recipes for Learning*. Englewood Cliffs, NJ: Prentice Hall, Inc., 1972.

Cole, A.; Haas, C.; Heller, E.; and Weinberger, B. *A Pumpkin in a Pear Tree: Creative Ideas for 12 Months of Holiday Fun*. Boston, Toronto: Little, Brown and Company, 1976.

Hendrix, John and Lela. *Experiential Education: EX-ED*. Nashville, TN: Abingdon, 1975.

Vienna. *Create & Celebrate*. New York: Morehouse Barlow, 1972.

Reflection

Burke, C., ed. *Loneliness*. Winona, MN: St. Mary's College Press, 1970.

Burke, C., and Cummins, R., eds. *Searching for Meaning*. Winona, MN: St. Mary's College Press, 1970.

Collins, M.; Savary, L.; and Carter, J. *Ritual and Life*. Winona, MN: St. Mary's College Press, 1970.

Reynolds, Si, ed. *Careless Potato*. Winona, MN: St. Mary's College Press, 1973.

Savary, L.; Carter, J.; and Burke, C.; eds. *Shaping of Self*. Winona, MN: St. Mary's College Press, 1970.

Stories

Hall, Brian. *Nog's Vision*. New York: Paulist Press, 1973.

Hall, Brian. *The Wizard of Maldoone*. New York: Paulist Press, 1975.

Lionni, Leo. *Frederick*. New York: Pantheon Books, 1967. (Also available in film).

Lionni, Leo. *Pezzettino*. New York: Pantheon Books, 1975.

McDermott, Gerald. *Arrow to the Sun*. New York: Viking Press, 1975 (also in film).

McDermott, Gerald. *Anansi the Spider*. Garden City, NJ: Puffin Books, 1977.

Morse, Charles and Ann. *Whobody There*. Winona, MN: St. Mary's College Press, 1971.

Paulus, Trina. *Hope for the Flowers*. New York: Paulist Press, 1972.

Sendak, Maurice. *Where the Wild Things Are*. New York: Harper & Row, 1963.

Silverstein, Shel. *Where the Sidewalk Ends*. New York: Harper & Row, 1974.

Thomas, Marlo. *Free to Be You and Me*. New York: McGraw-Hill, 1974.

Williams, Margery. *The Velveteen Rabbit*. Garden City, NJ: Doubleday & Co.

Songbooks

American Favorite Ballads, Oak Publications.

Hymnal for Young Christians, F. E. L. Publications.

Joan Baez Songbook.

Little Boxes and Other Handmade Songs, Malvina Reynolds.

LP Records

Free to Be . . . You and Me, by Marlo Thomas and Friends, 1972. Bell Records, 1776 Broadway, New York, NY 10019.

Hi God! (includes "Get in Touch with the Way You Feel"), by Carey Landry, 1973. North American Liturgy Resources, 300 East McMillan Street, Cincinnati, OH 45219.

Joy Is Like the Rain, by the Medical Mission Sisters. Avant Garde Records, Inc., 250 West 57th Street, New York, NY 10019.

Peter, Paul & Mommy, by Peter, Paul & Mary. Warner Bros-Seven Arts Records.

Other Sources

Magazine:

Mushroom Family. Published by Fredrick C. Doscher, P. O. Box 12572, Pittsburgh, PA.

Films:

Insights. Virginia Satir, author and consultant; John Goodell, producer and director. Order from:
Manitou Productions, Inc.
4900 IDS Center
Minneapolis, MN 55402

A Better Place to Stand. Virginia Satir, author and consultant; John Goodell, producer and director. Order from:
Manitou Productions, Inc.
4900 IDS Center
Minneapolis, MN 55402